Women Inspired: Sunshine Coast 2023

www.womeninspired.com.au
© Jaya McIntyre and Roxanne McCarty-O'Kane 2023

The creators wish to acknowledge some stories featured in this book shares women's experiences with mental health, domestic violence, sexual abuse and eating disorders. Please read with care. If you are triggered by any content, please seek professional support through a service such as Lifeline 13 11 14, White Ribbon Australia 1800 737 732, or endED 0407 592 932.

Photography by Jaya McIntyre of Empire Art Photography www.empireartphotography.com.au
Stories by Roxanne McCarty-O'Kane www.roxannewriter.com.au
Editing by Melinda Uys www.melindauys.com

Printed by Clark & Mackay www.clark-mackay.com.au

ISBN: 978-0-6450957-4-6

A catalogue record for this book is available from the National Library of Australia

WOMEN INSPIRED

n a world where pain and adversity are all too common, stories of hope and inspiration have the power to transform lives. Every person's life is a tapestry of experiences, both uplifting and challenging. Sharing our stories allows us to connect with others on a deeply human level, reminding them that they are not alone in their struggles.

It is by acknowledging and owning our mental and physical scars that we find the courage to let ourselves be seen, and in doing so, we create a ripple effect of healing and growth. When others see themselves in you, your story becomes a source of comfort, guidance, and motivation, providing a roadmap for others who may be navigating similar paths.

WHEN WE REVEAL OUR VULNERABILITIES, WE INSPIRE HOPE BY SHOWING THAT STRENGTH CAN EMERGE FROM THE MOST PAINFUL CIRCUMSTANCES.

It is by no means an easy feat to lay yourself bare, it takes bravery to step out of the shadows and allow yourself to be seen, flaws and all. The women in this book are warrior women in their own industries, fields of expertise and areas of passion. Even though society teaches us to conceal our pain, to present an image of strength and invulnerability, the women in these pages are standing tall and owning their unmasked truth.

Through our openness, we dismantle the walls that isolate us and cultivate a community of support. Sharing our stories is an opportunity to find meaning and purpose in even the most challenging moments whilst acknowledging the growth and transformation we have experienced as a result of our lived experience. By illustrating that healing is possible, we inspire others to embark on their own transformative journeys. What a legacy! And the best part is, we all have the ability to leave a legacy by simply sharing what we know.

AMANDA RICHENS

"The secret of change is to focus all of your energy, not on fighting the old, but on building the new."
- *Socrates*

AIMEE RUSSELL

"Strength doesn't come from winning. It comes from struggles and hardship. Everything that you go through prepares you for the next level."
- Germany Kent

ALLYCIA STAPLES

"You have one life... so go and live it!"
- *Lagertha in Vikings*

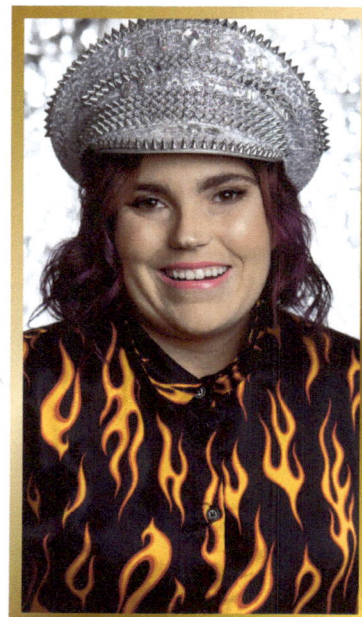

AMANDA STEVENS

"A rising tide lifts all boats."
- *John F Kennedy*

AMY BENNETT

"Get curious, not furious."
- Anonymous

ANGELA WILLIAMS

"From everyone to whom much is given, much will be required."
- *Luke 12:48.*

AMANDA RICHENS

SERIAL ENTREPRENEUR

thrive on the thrill of creating and developing business and welcome new opportunities to challenge myself. This trait was passed down to me from my father, who made the bold decision to move from the UK to Australia at a young age, in search of better opportunities and a higher quality of life for his soon to be growing family.

RISKS CAN BE SINK OR SWIM AT TIMES, BUT I DON'T MIND JUMPING INTO THAT OCEAN.

In my toughest moments, I simply have to remember one thing: Breathe. Once I have centred myself, I then reflect and remind myself, *we are only dealt with, what we can deal with.* Remembering that powerful mantra allows me to focus on creating a plan to find a solution. This mindset has served me well both personally and professionally, even in the darkest of days.

My life changed drastically in my early thirties when my two-year-old son Zac was diagnosed with Acute Lymphoblastic Leukemia. As a single mother, I had to confront not only my son's illness but the loss of my home, career, income, and what felt like, my sanity. But in that moment of despair, I realised that everything I had lost was replaceable, except for my son.

I picked myself up and began studying for a new career while caring for Zac in the hospital. In 2009, he went into remission, and I have practiced gratitude daily ever since to keep myself grounded. Zac is now a healthy, happy and strong 21-year-old living and loving his life on the Sunshine Coast with his mates, our blended family and thriving career.

My willingness to take risks has led to a successful career spanning more than 20 years in the fast-moving consumer goods, food and beverage industry. I have held my own in what is largely a male-dominated industry and have worked with reputable local and global companies. I excel at building long-lasting, mutually beneficial relationships as a National Business Development Manager within the travel, accommodation, pub and leisure channels.

One of my recent accomplishments was securing a national preferred agreement between Nestle Professional and Dilmah Tea. This allowed me to visit the Dilmah School of Tea in Sri Lanka and spend time with the Dilmah family. I feel a strong connection to them as one of the many charities Dilmah Tea support in Australia is My Room Children's Cancer Charity in Australia, a cause that is close to my heart.

I'm not afraid of jumping into new opportunities nor the hard work that comes with it, and have several business ventures including Noosa Melting Moments which specialises in décor fragrances and Sand Between Your Toes (SBYT), the brainchild of my husband and I. SBYT is a lifestyle brand that includes a clothing line, 4WD Crew expeditions catering for all levels and SBYT Events providing tools for coping with change.

I love the adrenaline rush that comes when you throw your time and energy into creating something new and exciting in business. It helps me to evolve everyday and there is no fear that I will gather moss from inaction!

I am excited for the new opportunities that lie ahead!

https://www.linkedin.com/in/amanda-richens-a38b2064
noosameltingmoments.com.au
sandbetweenyourtoes.com.au

AIMEE RUSSELL

OWNER OF AIMEE PROVENCE HIGH TEA PARLOUR

I spent my early years in a quaint village in Hertfordshire, UK. Our house was surrounded by picturesque fields, and my siblings and I had ducks, chickens and goats as beloved companions. However, when my parents divorced, we had to downsize to a mobile home. During this time, I gained a deep appreciation for wise financial management: every penny was needed to meet our most basic needs.

During my childhood, my mother had a series of romantic partners. This brought considerable instability to our lives, distress which was compounded when I was sexually abused at the age of nine by one of these individuals. My ordeal was aggravated by cruel school bullies, my struggle with dyslexia and mixed Persian heritage. By the time I was 14, the cumulative weight of these experiences had taken such a toll on my wellbeing that, at times, I contemplated ending my own life.

Significant gaps in my schooling made further education unattainable. Instead, at 19 I became an exotic dancer in an exclusive establishment, mingling with affluent businessmen, footballers and celebrities.

IT WAS DURING THIS PHASE OF MY LIFE THAT I TRULY EMBRACED MY INDEPENDENCE AND HARNESSED MY POWER AS A WOMAN.

With these remarkable earnings, I made a significant stride towards financial stability by purchasing my first property. In 2009 I arrived in Australia with my partner, keen to pursue a new chapter. I studied interior design in Sydney, and in 2012 we were overjoyed to welcome our daughter, Zara, into the world.

Everything seemed to align perfectly, and four years later we moved to the Sunshine Coast where I purchased a failed business in Buderim. With determination, lots of hard work and careful attention to detail, I transformed it into a delightful High Tea Parlour.

When I reflect on those early days of Aimee Provence, I'm filled with a profound sense of peace and accomplishment. Lacking familial support, Zara would accompany me, occasionally throwing a tantrum amidst my efforts to bake everything from scratch and prepare coffees. It warms my heart to see her growing fondness for the parlour: now she aspires to become a barista!

While I have certainly made my fair share of mistakes as a businesswoman, they have been overshadowed by numerous successes. One triumph was the introduction of high tea hamper deliveries during the Covid-19 lockdowns. They were so well-received that they've become a permanent offering. Looking ahead, the prospect of franchising Aimee Provence fills me with boundless excitement as we enter the next stage of growth.

Each time life knocks me down, I summon the strength to rebuild, driven by my unwavering dedication to my daughters. After two heartbreaking miscarriages, our rainbow baby, Amelia, arrived in late 2022, filling our lives with immeasurable joy. I am profoundly grateful that their childhood is filled with laughter, limitless opportunities, and a sense of wonder.

Every day, I continue to grapple with my own challenges of anxiety and depression. They cast a heavy toll on my life, testing my resilience and strength. However, these difficult struggles shape us into stronger individuals, capable of incredible things.

www.aimeeprovence.com.au

ALLYCIA STAPLES

SINGER, DANCER, CHOREOGRAPHER AND ACTRESS

Viking Queen Lagertha is strong and fierce, she doesn't take no for an answer and she's a warrior. When I think of how I would tell my life story, it would be in the form of Lagertha, from the popular show *Vikings*.

I am a quadruple-threat performer and have been dancing, choreographing, singing and acting my whole life. I have a deletion on chromosome 18 and I consider it an absolute gift.

I have danced to so many awesome songs as part of the Sunshine Troupe, a collective of creatives with disabilities. We began performing together 14 years ago, and I am one of the four remaining OG's. Success with them is one of my greatest joys. I love that we perform at major events on the Sunshine Coast and have created some amazing theatrical works. We have performed so many times that I can't count them all!

One of the biggest shows was for over three hundred people at the STEPS Winter Ball, but my favourite was a short drama and dance piece at Queen Street Mall in Brisbane. It was the first time I choreographed a jazz contemporary style dance and it was to Mans Zelmerlow's song 'Heroes'. We performed as part of the **Arts and Cultural Program for the INAS Global Games**. It was like the whole street stopped what they were doing to watch us and I thought *Wow, we actually did that!* It was phenomenal.

I have performed with mainstream groups and was part of True Grit in Sydney in 2022, where I worked with dancers from the Australian Ballet and performed in the Utzon Room at Sydney Opera House. I have been a Young Achiever finalist and represented the Sunshine Coast in New Caledonia at the Handicapable Conference, performing as a solo dancer.

My love of music is also channelled through The Outsiders, a six-piece band I joined six years ago. I play the tambourine and sing. We were featured on Rope TV and have recorded music videos for our original songs 'Show Me The Way', which featured a rap by the top bomb MC Wheels, and 'Live Our Lives', which is my number one favourite.

I am driven by my love for performance and seeing what I might achieve next.

WHENEVER THINGS GET TOUGH, I TELL MYSELF, 'LIFE IS GOOD, KEEP GOING, YOU NEVER KNOW WHAT MIGHT HAPPEN NEXT – ANYTHING COULD HAPPEN!'

My life is pretty exciting! I am in my third year of studying at Bus Stop Film School and I work with self-advocacy group Loud and Clear and with Bush Kids as a resource assistant.

I was a founding member of the Aha Ensemble; we had residencies with La Boite, Metro Arts, the Institute of Modern Art and Judith Wright Centre in 2022. I am also developing my own theatrical work, a production called Be Lagertha, to tell my life story with great music, visuals and a few surprises.

This future show is from my heart and soul. I want people to know that I am a strong, fierce woman just like Lagertha. I want to show that even if you have a disability, you can take your message around the world! I have a big life and there is nothing I cannot do.

www.sunshinetroupe.org.au

AMANDA STEVENS

AWARD-WINNING INTERNATIONAL KEYNOTE SPEAKER, AUTHOR, BUSINESS OWNER, CHARITY AMBASSADOR

still have no idea how it happened, but in November 2021 I was fighting for my life. Septicaemia, a blood infection, had seized hold of me and after several days in intensive care, I was facing severe amputation and even death. To pull through, I focused on the bravest thought I could in each moment.

Not that I'd recommend the experience, but it demonstrated perfectly how even though you may not be physically strong, you always have the choice to be mentally brave. For me, septicaemia crystallised what was really important and solidified how living a life of purpose is the greatest gift you can give yourself and others.

I'VE LIVED WITH A LITTLE MORE VELOCITY SINCE THEN – TAKING THE HOLIDAYS, DRINKING THE WINE, EATING THE CHOCOLATE.

Ultimately you have one life, so why not do what you love? It sounds so simple, but it's not simplistic.

The most interesting 'personal development' course I ever did was going through IVF. I suffered from premature ovarian failure at 36 and after selling my award-winning Sydney-based marketing and research agency and launching onto the speaking circuit in 2010, I was ready to have a child. I took all the potions, used all the lotions and stabbed myself with IVF drugs for a total of seven years... a Tony Robbins course is probably cheaper!

In the end, persistence overcame resistance. I learned patience and gratitude, powerful lessons in both life and business. My marriage ended when I was 10 weeks pregnant, so I went into motherhood with a *if it's going to be, it's up to me* attitude. Ollie arrived nine weeks premature; he had a rocky, uncertain start to life weighing just 1500 grams. He's the bravest, most resilient little human I know. I scooped him up and he travelled the world with me so I could continue to earn a great living, be with him almost fulltime and build a sense of awe and wonder in him from exposure to different environments and cultures. Ollie clocked up his 100th flight before he turned two!

I had a lot of help from my 'village' of nannies and a core group of strong, supportive women. Covid was debilitating for me, not only because it cut off my source of income, but I underestimated how hard it was not to do what I loved. I 'pirouetted' though, and created a digital marketing agency for speakers and a mastermind group to support them with their marketing. It's an example of my abundance mentality and collaborative approach to business, something which is also evident in my personal life.

A piece of equipment bought through the Running for Premature Babies charity helped save Ollie's life when he was in the Neonatal Intensive Care Unit. When I discovered NICUs rely heavily on external funding, I became the charity's Queensland ambassador. I had been training for a half-marathon when septicaemia struck, and doctors credit my recovery to a high baseline fitness. In a beautiful full-circle moment, Sophie Smith, the charity's founder, helped saved my son's life, and then also saved mine.

We are all braver than we give ourselves credit for. True resilience comes from little acts of bravery every day. They have a cumulative effect and you become capable of anything you put your mind to.

www.amandastevens.com.au

15

AMY BENNETT

AWARD-WINNING REAL ESTATE AGENT, HOST OF BEYOND THE SIGNBOARD PODCAST

When I left my highly lucrative corporate pharmaceutical career in Melbourne, my boss cried. Why? He was 20 years my senior and said he wished he had the courage to do the same.

I'd had a successful trajectory uncommon for women in that industry at the time, but I made a conscientious choice to come back to the Sunshine Coast in 2013. I needed more balance, connection and alignment in my life, and I was prepared to take a 60 per cent pay cut to do it. The first thing I did was dye my hair pink again. Immediately, I felt the real Amy begin to re-emerge.

As a single mother, my mum modelled the powers of strength and independence to me constantly. She worked two jobs, six days a week and volunteered on as many as five community committees at a time, yet she never compromised on quality time with me. Most importantly, Mum taught me the value of connection and giving back.

Courage runs in my blood. Passed down by a powerful lineage of Viking women, it gives me the strength to love my life of dichotomy. I'm analytical and constantly learning, but I'm spiritual and wear crystals in my bra. I'm nerdy and love a good game of Scrabble, but I also rock out in a hardcore moshpit. I have tattoos, pink hair and a pink house (a whimsical homage to the pink house of my childhood), but I am a consummate professional. I embrace it all because my zest for life is stronger than any attempt to minimise who I am.

PEOPLE SAY TO ME, 'I WISH I HAD THE COURAGE TO BE AS BOLD AS YOU,' AND MY RESPONSE IS ALWAYS, 'WHY DON'T YOU?'

Courage can take many different forms, from freedom to express your authentic self to trusting your intuition to start again at the bottom of the ladder. Bravery is also knowing your worth and creating boundaries. I put my entire heart and soul into whatever - and whoever - I commit to, and while I could easily work 24/7, I am a crusader against the belief that self-care is selfish. Exhaustion isn't a badge of honour.

I've learned how to say no and surround myself with inspirational people who are authentic, honest and vulnerable. I know when to tap out and have a quiet afternoon on the couch with a magazine, my pugs and my husband DB.

I gravitate to roles that feed my drive for connection and contribution. As McGrath Estate Agents' Operations & Marketing Manager since 2016, I've played an instrumental role in establishing the Community Giveback program, which has supported more than 200 local charities.

In 2021, I drew on all my reserves of courage to conquer my ultimate fear: jumping out of a plane. I'm a different person because of that 60-second freefall and when I was offered a role as an agent just weeks later, handing back my work car and a regular pay packet to take a chance once again did not phase me in the slightest!

I have won an award every year for the past six at the agency and with Mum, DB and a host of authentic and inspirational friends behind me, I know I'll continue to be unstoppable.

www.linkedin.com/in/amyvbennett

17

ANGELA WILLIAMS

AUTHOR OF EXTRAVAGANT LIFE TO EXTRAVAGANT LOVE, CO-HOST OF THE GOLD DIGGERS PODCAST.

love a bit of tongue-in-cheek humour, so when the time came to think of a name for the podcast I launched with my good friend Beck, I wanted to call it The Gold Diggers, knowing full well what it represents. You see, the title is a perfect play on words for me. I am after all, the daughter of a British Lord and from one of the wealthiest families in England.

Gaining riches in life is considered the ultimate prize. People of wealth are admired, esteemed and viewed as role models with little consideration of their character. Yet, I know from experience that the real gold is not in what you have, but in who you are.

As a young mother, I was inspired to give back and founded a charity called Embrace which helped rescue and restore women working in prostitution, in particular street sex workers in Warwickshire. Needless to say, I learned a thing or two while walking the streets befriending those women.

Instead of the Hollywood glamourised portrayal of prostitution, I discovered a desperate world with many hidden faces. The women changed my life as I realised how beautiful and kind they were beneath the rags. Everyone has value, but most can't see the gold within themselves, they only see metaphorical rags.

WE MAKE JUDGEMENTS BASED ON APPEARANCES AND LIFESTYLE, BUT WHEN WE DARE TO DIG DEEPER AND LOOK BEYOND THE SURFACE, THAT'S WHEN WE DISCOVER THE REAL GOLD.

I wrote about my commitment to provide a voice for the Warwickshire sex workers and create a platform for people to look beyond labels in my 2021 book *Extravagant Life to Extravagant Love,* but the podcast has allowed Beck and I to go that step further. We uncover gold in everyday people every single week since we launched in June 2022.

We never truly know what will unfold; the episodes are unscripted and anything goes, which is exciting! One of us either knows the guest personally or has researched them before the show. The other co-host is completely in the dark and it is their job to pose questions to see whether they can excavate the same gold the host 'in the know' discovered or find something else that is just as precious!

I am continually inspired by the resilience and strength in people who come through the studio believing they haven't done much in life. They may have endured real hardships and just thought it was normal life, not realising what they have done is extraordinary. I love to show people their value so they can truly understand their worth, and everyone leaves feeling encouraged and empowered.

Although I am no stranger to the microphone, having delivered countless public speaking presentations, as an MC at events and host at charitable functions, the podcast has been the perfect training ground to hone my interview skills in preparation for future projects and opportunities in media.

There is so much more to life than possessions and when we shift our focus off trying to keep up with The Jones' and instead benchmark our life on finding the gold in people, we will live much happier and fulfilled lives. Now, there's the real gold!

www.thegolddiggers.com.au

ANNETTE O'CONNOR

"Spread love everywhere you go. Let no one come to you without leaving happier."
- *Mother Teresa*

ASHLEE JENSEN

"Weather the storm, there is beauty amongst the chaos."
- Carla Beth Green

CASS CONNOLLY

"We do not need magic to transform our world. We carry all of the power we need inside ourselves already."
- *J.K Rowling*

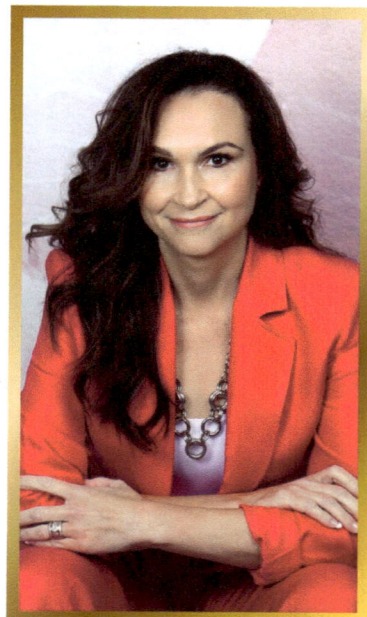

EBONY PARKE

"Surround yourself with people who are only going to lift you higher."
- Oprah Winfrey

EUFRASIA GAGLIARDO

"All for one and one for all."
- Alexandre Dumas

FABE KEILY

"Life is very simple, what we give out we get back."
- Louise Hay

ANNIE O'CONNOR

SONOGRAPHER, AWARD-WINNING BUSINESSWOMAN, CANCER SURVIVOR

2018 was certainly a year I would like to have skipped. Just the year prior, life seemed to be in perfect balance. My husband and I had sold the award-winning business we'd built over 23 years, First Class Functions, and we had just started to enjoy a more leisurely lifestyle with our children. I continued with my passion of working as a sonographer two days a week at a Sunshine Coast private radiology practice. Everything seemed rosy.

Then, in February 2018, I was diagnosed with breast cancer following a routine mammogram. People think working in the medical field gives you an advantage because of your knowledge, but sometimes it works in reverse. Once the sonographer measured the tumour, I knew immediately it was large enough to be an advanced cancer. I sat in the car park wondering *how long have I got?* It was beyond confronting: now I knew firsthand the struggle patients go through.

THAT WAS THE ONLY PITY PARTY I ALLOWED MYSELF. MY TYPE OF CANCER HAD AN 80 PER CENT SURVIVAL RATE: THERE WAS NO WAY I WAS GOING TO BE THE 20 PER CENT.

I had a mastectomy and began a six-month course of chemotherapy and radiation. Two weeks before completing my treatment, I received an unexpected late night call: my eldest son Jack had been hit by a car while standing on the side of Eumundi-Noosa Road. *He'll be taken to the hospital, everything will be okay,* I told myself, even though my heart was in my throat as we waited for more information.

My son Harry had been waiting for his older brother to come home to play together on the Xbox. I was upstairs when Harry answered the door to the police and I will never forget the feeling of utter devastation as I saw him slump against the wall, slide down and hit his head once he found out his 18-year-old brother had been killed. That agonising memory plays over and over in my head.

The moment I realised Jack was really gone; cancer became more like a bad headache in comparison to the unfathomable heartbreak of losing my son. It was hard to support my husband, three other children and Jack's friends, who reached out for comfort, when I could not grasp the enormity of my own grief.

The experiences of 2018 inspired me to take on additional challenges in an attempt to renew my confidence and self-assurance. I started a Master's degree in Health Administration in 2020, hoping it might improve my chemo brain and provide diversional grief therapy, but I deferred after only two weeks. I'm very driven and don't like to fail at anything, so I re-enrolled in 2021 and began a new job at the Sunshine Coast University Hospital.

I know there are still so many things to be grateful for. I was on my may to work when a song played on the radio. Hopelessly triggered, I arrived, cheeks streaked with mascara. I couldn't stop crying but afterwards, I felt a sense of peace and calm. I no longer felt the pressure to reclaim the same level of happiness I'd had before we lost Jack. I had been pushing and pushing, but in that moment, I realised it was an unrealistic pursuit. Finally, I felt free to find a new level of happiness.

https://www.linkedin.com/in/annette-oconnor-b0949729/

ASHLEE JENSEN

AWARD-WINNING FILMMAKER, WRITER, DIRECTOR AND FOUNDER OF THE COAST COLLECTIVE

Glossy productions with actor/models, fluffy scripts or huge CGI budgets just don't do it for me. I need real. I need raw. I need stories that start conversations around taboo subjects. I need diversity of voice. Most importantly, I need people to watch my movies and never feel like they are 'less than'.

I carried that not-good-enough feeling throughout my childhood, suffering ten years of incessant bullying because of my weight. I'd been prescribed anabolic steroids at the age of five to combat chronic asthma and eczema.

I had such an uncomfortable relationship with my body that my diaries from that era were filled with horrific, disgusting things about myself. I went cold turkey off my medication at 15 and to my surprise, every single person treated me differently as the weight fell off. I finally felt accepted and seen.

This dramatic shift led to an obsession with controlling what I ate. I was so terrified of going back to being ostracised that I descended into a decade-long spiral that severely compromised my health. Despite the extremes I went to, there was a voice within that whispered *life is so much bigger than this.* There was a fire inside me that no longer wanted to be defined by an eating disorder. With a heck of a lot of soul searching, sheer determination and willpower, I began an ongoing health and spiritual journey that has seen me heal my trauma.

That experience gave me such a great depth of understanding, compassion and empathy. I think these are superpowers within themselves, but when combined with my storytelling, I became invincible.

LIKE MANY WOMEN IN THE INDUSTRY, I HAVE OPENED MY OWN DOORS BECAUSE I WAS SICK OF HAVING THEM SLAMMED IN MY FACE.

I'm a firm believer in never putting your dreams in someone else's hands. Instead, I've built networks with people who appreciate me as a leader and a visionary, and have helped me make amazing things happen. As a result of positive collaboration, I've walked red carpets around the world and accepted multiple awards since I released my first feature film in 2014.

I am on the path now to receiving an autism diagnosis, which comes with a swirl of emotions: the relief to have this key to understanding myself on a deeper level, but also sadness for the soul-destroying years I'd spent people-pleasing and masking who I was just to fit in.

I am now kinder to myself and recognise I'm still a work in progress. I have a daily routine that helps me nurture a mindset that I can take on anything! It involves journaling what I appreciate in my life and career, listening to industry podcasts, engaging in artistic expression, daydreaming so I can visualise a story or project and grounding myself in nature to replenish my energy.

Through all of this, I have found the self-belief to hold true to my ambitions and dreams despite the negative people who pop up in life. I no longer care if someone doesn't grasp the magnitude of my goals or understand what I'm capable of, because I surround myself with people who do.

www.ashleetamarajensen.com.au
www.thecoastcollective.com.au

CASS CONNOLLY

SENIOR MORTGAGE BROKER AT YOUR MORTGAGE COACH

"I t's not my problem, you can pay it." It was simple as that. My abusive nine-year relationship ended in 2000, and my partner refused to pay off the loans we'd acquired during our relationship. I was left with nothing but a mountain of debt and a suitcase of clothes. Staring down the barrel of bankruptcy was mortifying, particularly since I was pursuing a career in the banking sector.

Declaring bankruptcy would jeopardise my career, but I was determined I would not be beaten. I sold our house to clear the debt, started from scratch, rebuilt myself and forged a career in finance.

Having started as a clerk in a small community Credit Union, I had worked my way up and hit a ceiling I could not break through. I found a passion for loans, but when a position came up, I was overlooked in favour of a male teller with no experience because I was told, "The reality is, people don't deal with women as well as men when it comes to finance."

I thrive on a challenge and get the most gratification from overcoming an obstacle. Needless to say, as soon as a more open-minded branch manager arrived at the bank, I put my case forward and become the first female Loans Officer.

TELL ME I CAN'T DO SOMETHING AND I'LL BE DETERMINED TO PROVE YOU WRONG.

I found strength in my independence and began to gravitate towards helping single women own their own home, especially those who had suffered from financial abuse. They are often turned away by other brokers, and I knew firsthand how crucial building financial independence can be.

My star continued to rise within the industry. I managed a financial advising and mortgage broking firm at 24 and two years later, became the youngest ever Bank Manager for a large bank. Lending was my passion though, and I moved back to loans. It is simultaneously the most rewarding and frustrating job, because policies and lending criteria are constantly changing, but I will always find a way to help my clients achieve their goals.

An unexpected connection with John, an old school mate, in 2001 saw us marry that same year. He is my greatest champion. He keeps me safe, drives me, holds me and loves me for all of my perfect imperfections. We are a team like no other, without pink or blue belts; I put the Ikea flat packs together and he does the washing.

John and I have three beautiful children and life was on an even keel until two bowel obstructions and resection surgeries over two years left my body attacking itself when I was 36. My family have been my rock through it all and I am so grateful that I was able to dig deep and carry on. It's just the way I do things.

I thrive on a challenge and remain committed to helping people who really need life-changing loans. I dedicate my spare time to Fab Femme Finance, a platform that provides women hope, education and a pathway so they can find financial security. I share a message of hope that no matter what has happened in your financial world, you can always get back on your feet with the right support in your corner.

www.yourmortgagecoach.com.au

EBONY PARKE

AWARD–WINNING NATIONAL SALES AND MARKETING DIRECTOR AT 92.7 MIX FM AND 91.9 SEA FM

My daily alarm clock as a child was dad turning the radio on. Radio has always been a part of my life, but I found a whole new passion for it when I started working in the industry in 2003 at 92.7 MIX FM and 91.9 SEA FM.

After studying business and starting out on reception at the station, I moved into the role of airtime scheduling manager within 12 months. This was my first taste of behind the scenes radio, one most listeners never even think about. It was mind blowing and I was hooked.

I was in that role for 13 years, which saw many life-changing moments; marriage, the birth of two daughters and travelling. But my love for radio and the people who have that community connection never wavered.

At the end of 2017, I pitched a new role to our CEO within the National Sales Department of our business, one where I could see growth, opportunity, and use my previous 14 years of industry knowledge and contacts to an advantage.

COURAGE HAS ALWAYS BEEN A DEFINING TRAIT OF MINE, AND I HAVE NEVER CONSIDERED IT A DAUNTING TASK TO ADVOCATE FOR CHANGE.

I'm a go-getter and I tackle challenges head on driven by an unwavering determination to achieve my goals. I don't sit and procrastinate on significant tasks. Instead, I take a proactive approach of meticulous planning, conduct thorough research, and willingly seek assistance or additional resources to deliver above expectation.

When I embarked on my radio career, the Sunshine Coast lacked female representation in management positions; it was challenging to envision myself as a leader. But naturally over time, this changed and in January 2022, I was promoted to National Sales and Marketing Director. It is a testament to how opportunities present when hard work, loyalty, dedication, and determination are recognised.

I'd always secretly wanted to win a coveted Australian Commercial Radio Award: for the radio industry this is a pinnacle of success. My first opportunity arose when I won Best Sales Promotion (non-metro) with 91.9 SEA FM and Bendigo Bank's 'Great Australian Dream' campaign in 2021. The results we attained from this campaign were truly extraordinary and the client's return on investment exceeded every anticipation, leaving an unforgettable imprint of success. The subsequent year brought another victory in the same category, where I won an award for the exceptional Brewed by Eu campaign, a collaboration between 92.7 MIX FM and Eumundi Brewery.

I truly believe that as a leader, you should foster an environment where mistakes are embraced without shame and support individuals when they occur. Together we work towards effective problem-solving and resolutions. Open communication and strong relationships, both within the team and with our clients, has been the key to running a cohesive, collaborative, and ultimately successful department. I am so grateful to be working with some of the smartest and most creative minds in the radio industry.

https://www.linkedin.com/in/ebony-parke-362607158/

EUFRASIA GAGLIARDO

OWNER MAR GRA, AUTHOR

"The Sunshine Coast is like a sleeping beauty, but she will wake up, and I want to be part of it," my husband John assured the people who tried to talk us out of setting up a business in Moffat Beach in the eighties. They had no idea how driven and determined we could be.

It was an exciting and daunting time of our lives. We had moved from Italy to start from scratch and experience life on a new continent. I grew up in Massawa, known as 'the pearl of the red sea,' a port city of Eritrea. After I married John, we experienced many different cultures and ways of life as we raised our three children, living in Africa and Europe before landing on the white sandy shores of Australia.

John was right, the Sunshine Coast is now becoming cosmopolitan and our family has been part of that evolution over the last three decades. I am very proud of my daughter Mariangela and sons Luigi and Johnpaul. We have always been a very tight knit family and have done everything together in business and in life.

Through Mar Gra we have helped put a touch of class into homes and elevated resorts and hospitality venues by using the best that nature has to offer with our marble and granite. We do not just give people benchtops; we give them works of art made by God, and He went wild with some of the colours!

Staying in business for almost 40 years hasn't come easy, but every day is a clean slate and you never know where the day will take you. When we started the business, marble and granite were not well known as benchtops; people knew about sandstone in the construction industry as a building material, but not as a finishing product. We had to educate the market about the benefits of using a natural material that stands the test of time... just look at the Colosseum!

We had to build our reputation, build demand in the market and pave the way for those who came after us: we did all of the 'hard yakka'. There were nights when I started to believe the people who told us we were crazy, but if you don't have faith, you won't go anywhere. I am a very determined, resilient and stubborn person, so if I have a goal, I will do everything I can to attain it.

I BELIEVE AS LONG AS YOU PUT IN HONEST WORK, YOU CAN BE BENT BY CHALLENGES WITHOUT EVER LETTING THEM BREAK YOU.

If you have a dream, don't ever give up. If you really want it, just go for it. For years I put my family and our work ahead of my dream of writing a book, until I found all my short stories and handwritten chapters and decided that it was my turn to do something for myself.

I went for that dream and released my first book, *Living on the Pearl of the Red Sea,* in 2021. It is dedicated to the people I met in Eritrea during the first two decades of my life and how I was moulded by these interactions. My next goals are to travel more for pleasure and write as many books as I can... I know I can make these dreams happen too! Who knows what will be next?

www.margra.com.au

FABE KEILY

CEO AND FOUNDER EMPOWERING WOMEN NETWORK, MANAGING DIRECTOR WOMEN'S LIFESTYLE EXPO

As I stepped up to the solid pine board in front of me, I read the message I'd scrawled on it earlier that day, "If I can break through this pine board, I can break through financially." I had no idea when I signed up for an investment seminar in 1998, that so much would be dedicated to personal development, but there I was, preparing to do something I never thought was possible.

Highly competitive, I'd grown up with five brothers, had always wanted to stick it to the boys, and even became the Sunshine Coast's first female surf lifesaver in 1979. And yet, the seminar had given me the opportunity to reflect. I'd carried unconscious self-limiting beliefs around what I could do, be, have or achieve.

Well, I smashed that pine board and found a new sense of self. I began to see opportunities where I had never dared look before.

I DEVELOPED THE B.E.A.R. FORMULA FOR SUCCESS: BELIEF + EDUCATION + ACTION = RESULTS. I USE THIS IN EVERY AREA OF MY LIFE.

Suddenly, nothing could stop me. I invested in property and small developments alongside my career in event management. I went back to the seminar as a volunteer before being becoming their national and international events manager. I also ran my own women's personal development conferences, helping thousands of women from 17 to 70 break through their own physical and metaphorical pine boards and go on to do incredible things.

The next major breakthrough occurred in 2006 when I stepped up to break a board in front of 600 people at our biggest event to date; I couldn't break it! I went upstairs and studied my reflection in the bathroom mirror. I noticed my posture was off and realised my focus was on a million other things, rather than the result I wanted. With a singular focus, I went back the following morning and broke it on the first attempt.

Six years later, I became a FIFO General Manager, flying between Melbourne headquarters and my family home on the Sunshine Coast for four years, overseeing huge financial education summits featuring the likes of Sir Richard Branson, Arnold Schwarzenegger, Randi Zuckerberg and Mark Bouris. I took what I had learnt and the expertise I had gained, and in 2017 produced and distributed the *Real Woman Magazine* into the Virgin Business and VIP Lounges across Australia. This publication was brimming with empowerment for women in the areas of mindset, health, finance, business, career, lifestyle and travel.

It wasn't long before I came back to the power of a singular focus and my passion for helping women move through self-sabotage and succeed. In response to the global pandemic, I created the Empowering Women Network: I believe if you can't back yourself, surround yourself with people who will back you until you can. I couple this global 'free to join' membership driven network, with the Women's Lifestyle Expo to help businesswomen profit from their passion.

The pine board I broke through 25 years ago is mounted like a trophy in my office, and every time I think I can't do something, it reminds me that the only person holding me back is me… *Anything is possible, if I believe!*

www.fabekeily.com

GAYLE FORBES

"Live deliberately and actively and make your religion kindness."
- Gayle Forbes

JESSICA MCILVEEN

"Lose what needs to be lost to find what needs to be found."
-        Unknown

JORDYN JAMES

"The most alluring thing a woman can have is confidence."
-   Beyonce

KYLIE CHIVERS

"Don't look back, you're not going that way…"
- Mary Engelbreit

LEAH POLWARTH

"Every new beginning, comes from some other beginning's end."
- Semisonic, 'Closing Time.'

LISA CURRY

"Throw me to the wolves and I will come back leading the pack."
- Seneca

GAYLE FORBES

CO-FOUNDER OF ENDED

In the dimly lit hospital room, I adjusted the blanket under my daughter's chin. Settling into the chair beside her, I prepared for yet another long and worrisome night. As a parent supporting a child battling an enduring eating disorder, each passing year saw more health complications and co-occurring conditions arose, further ensnaring her. A nurse came in for a routine check-up and saw me awkwardly perched in the chair and as she fussed over me, I burst into tears. *I'm being seen!* So many people forget entire families are traumatised by watching their loved ones battle this invisible demon.

Through my lens, my daughter seemed like a happy, healthy, confident and capable young lady. When she began showing signs of eating issues and maladaptive behaviours at 14, professionals merely addressed the surface-level issues. I tried to stay positive and normalise everything, but hindsight and wisdom are wonderful things. My daughter turned to drugs and alcohol to numb her pain, all the while, I fluctuated between fear and utter devastation, and feeling like a strong, protective lioness.

We found ourselves caught in a never-ending cycle: even though we could help her become medically stable and manage her mental health, if she couldn't thrive in the community, she would inevitably return to hospital. I still carry grief that I never experienced any rites of passage with my daughter. She was either unwell or unavailable for them. I know it must pale in comparison to her grief.

My husband Mark and I saw familiar faces in the hospital hallways, but instead of connecting, we'd cast our eyes down and carry on. Patients and caregivers were also addressed separately. There was no collaboration and so many people suffered in isolation. My daughter was 21 by the time we connected with 11 parents for a six-week program through the Queensland Hospital and Health Service. Mark and I invited them to continue to meet at our Buddina home and we created an open, safe, nonjudgmental space for caregivers to talk openly about fears, frustrations and anxieties without raising the eyebrows of a medical practitioner or psychologist.

THE VISION GREW TO EXPAND THIS CONNECTION TO PATIENTS AND LINK HOLISTIC RECOVERY COACHES INTO THE MEDICAL SYSTEM: WE FOUNDED ENDED IN 2016.

While Mark is the ideas person who maximises opportunities, I am the woman on the ground. I listen to the pain, the confusion, the mistrust, the tiredness, the heartache, and the helplessness people feel when their loved one is unwell and there isn't a clear, quick road to recovery. It gives me every motivation to show them there is hope.

We spent years pouring our heart and soul into securing funding and collaborative partnerships to build an Australian-first holistic residential facility on the Sunshine Coast. Everything was on track, but the vision unexpectedly changed for our larger partners. Mark and I made the heartbreaking decision to walk away from our dream in 2020 to ensure we could hold our heads high. We will always advocate for equality and justice in treatment.

endED continues at a grassroots level and we have established the House of Hope to rebuild our vision for a holistic healing environment with equitable access. My daughter inspires that vision every day. She is still on this earth fighting to understand and be understood. Her strength and conviction to live a life that she deserves, not one determined for her by her current state of mental and physical health, is inspiring to me.

www.ended.org.au

JESSICA MCILVEEN

DEGREE-QUALIFIED SOCIAL WORKER, NEURO LINGUISTIC PROGRAMMING MASTER PRACTITIONER, TIMELINE THERAPIST, HYPNOTHERAPIST, CHILD YOGA THERAPIST, FOUNDER OF THE HAPPY HOME NETWORK

felt defeated as I put one foot painstakingly in front of the other to enter an abandoned Spanish village located along The Camino trail. My vision of conquering the 825 kilometre pilgrimage from St Jean Pied de Port in the French Pyrenees to the Cathedral of Santiago de Compostela in Spain was as shattered as my legs.

I was young and fit, so thought I'd be able to smash through this adventure with minimal preparation; two weeks walking on the flat streets of Jersey, an island off the coast of France to be precise. But nearly 300 kilometres down and ten days in, frustration, aching muscles and sleep deprivation all got on top of me. I had a meltdown.

I was physically and mentally done, but there wasn't a soul around to ask for help. I expected a tumbleweed to roll through the main street at any moment as I hobbled around, hoping desperately for some sign of life.

The pain in my legs was excruciating and just when I thought there was no way I could walk any further, a young woman appeared. *She must be my guardian angel!* She may have thought she was offering me a simple lift, but the fact is, she saved my life that day.

I CAME AWAY WITH A POWERFUL UNDERSTANDING: THE UNIVERSE HAS YOUR BACK.

Before attempting The Camino, I had quit my job as a Brisbane-based social worker over frustration with systemic restrictions and decided I'd live in Italy for a few years. But once I was there, I realised very quickly that Italy wasn't going to save me from myself.

I spent two weeks on a friend's couch in London recovering from the trek. With uninterrupted space to be inspired, when I thought of the freedom of starting my own business and bringing harmony and connection back into family homes through yoga and teaching mind-body cohesion, I had a complete knowing. I'm talking full body goosebumps.

My next adventure began in 2018, when I became a businesswoman, launched Kids Yoga Therapy and evolved into a leading parent coach, speaker and researcher. I rebranded to the Happy Home Network and the business continued to thrive, but in 2022 I felt a sense of unease creep back in.

When I married Chaz, the love of my life, in 2023 he opened me up to new ways of being. While I thought I was living a life of freedom with my business, I was in fact still limited. I felt trapped by the misery and heaviness of the marketing content I created in order to work with the families I felt I was destined to help. I felt restricted by society's expectations of what it meant to be 'professional'. I didn't want to wear a suit jacket when I'm a casual kinda gal who would rather not even wear a bra. I was ready to come back to my authentic self.

I'm excited to step boldly forward and be a beginner again because self-belief is like a well-used muscle and unlike my legs, it will never wear out. After all, the universe rewards the brave and I can feel something forming, just out of my vision, that holds the next adventure.

www.jessicamcilveen.com

JORDYN JAMES

OWNER OF BURLESQUE L'AMOUR

S ome people take a lifetime to find their calling... I found mine when I was four. **Music felt incredible in my body, and I was drawn to beat and movement from that moment on.**

Two years later, I told Mum I wanted to be a dance teacher and even presented a design layout of my dream dance studio to my primary teacher as part of a school project.

Dance allows me to step into an alter-ego for the duration of a song or a performance, liberating different sides of myself.

I never detoured from the vision my six-year-old self conjured up. I launched my first business, Elevation Dance and Fitness, in 2009. I ran classes for children from my former high school hall and introduced classes for adults with a disability.

When *Burlesque* hit the big screen in 2010, I began to learn the sensual dance form. Four years later, I rebranded to Burlesque L'Amour and switched to adults only classes so I could focus on empowering women through dance.

My first 'studio' was in my parents' garage in 2014. I had just twelve students. Now, I have a professional studio and HQ, host classes in five additional locations and have more than 450 women aged between 18 and 75 enrolled.

In my studio I encourage women to embrace various types of feminine energy, because burlesque isn't only sexual; it can be sensual, powerful and even comedic.

I SEE STRENGTH AND BEAUTY IN EVERY WOMAN WHO STEPS INTO BURLESQUE L'AMOUR. IT IS MY WISH THAT ONCE THEY SPEND TIME WITH ME AND THE LADIES, THEY SEE IT IN THEMSELVES TOO.

We connect through dance, but every woman comes to Burlesque L'Amour for something different; fitness, friendship, to rediscover femininity or overcome body image issues. It took me a long time to realise that something as humble as following my passion could change women's lives, but I've seen so many embrace self-love and grow in confidence through dance. They walk a bit taller once they know who they truly are. I mean, once you've performed on stage in all your glory, you really can do anything!

Our first show '50 Shades of Burlesque' in 2014 had a maximum of one hundred tickets. In 2022, a Stadium Cabaret collaboration with Neil Carr saw us take over the Sunshine Coast Stadium with over a thousand tickets and 450 dancers. Everything was supersized and it was incredible. Our performances have raised more than $40,000 for charities. I have been recognised as an Australian of the Year finalist in 2019 and was a Sunshine Coast Business Women's Network Awards finalist in 2021. But for me, the true reward is seeing women flourish and shine.

As much as I love the stage, under all the glitter and glam, I am a massive dork who loves to have fun and be silly. Every morning I drink from a mug that says, 'What would Beyoncé do?' and it makes me giggle.

No matter what anyone is going through, my door is always open. Every woman deserves to honour, love and find themselves and sometimes just being in a room once a week with like-minded women is all they need to do it.

www.burlesquelamour.com.au

KYLIE CHIVERS

PROFESSIONAL PROPERTY INVESTOR AND DEVELOPER, BUSINESSWOMAN, FOUNDER OF THE FEMININE CONNECTION

From an early age, I chose an ambitious path less travelled.

At just 15 years old, I bravely left school and ventured into the artistry of hairdressing. At 20, I had already taken my first steps into entrepreneurship, purchasing my own property and defying the odds to open my own salon. The fire within me continued to burn, leading me to the skies as a flight attendant, where I dedicated seven fulfilling years, during which time I immersed myself in property. After becoming a mother, I built on my property knowledge to create Aspire Housing Group, delivering over 1,000 affordable homes. Simultaneously, I grew my property investment portfolio which now comprises more than 60 homes. That success also came with heartache.

Despite three gruelling business legal battles, a heart-wrenching divorce marred by betrayal, and the physical challenge of losing my hair due to Alopecia, I remained steadfast. I refused to succumb to bitterness, instead embracing a year of self-discovery, where I empowered myself to build a new life for me and my three children. Through perseverance and resilience, I emerged triumphant.

It was at the age of 44 that I embarked on a life-altering global journey, immersing myself in the teachings of personal development luminary, Tony Robbins. In a moment of revelation during a female-only workshop, I was handed a pair of alluring booty pants and captivating stripper heels. Little did I know that this unexpected gesture would unlock a profound truth within me: I had unwittingly stifled my own femininity. My pursuit of achievement had cost me my marriage and I had neglected to revel in the joys of carefree abandon, playfulness, and sensuality.

This epiphany struck a chord within me, resonating with the shared experiences of countless women. We, who embody femininity at our core, often find ourselves operating predominantly in masculine energy, driven by fear, scarcity, and survival instincts. The stronger we become, the harder it is to let go. I intimately understand this struggle, for I have walked that path.

Motivated by my personal journey and a deep-seated desire to redefine and reclaim femininity, I established The Feminine Connection in 2023. It is dedicated to empowering women to embrace both their masculine and feminine energies. As a mentor, I guide women on a transformative journey, helping them master the delicate interplay between these energies and reignite their true essence.

IN THE MODERN WORLD, THE PURSUIT OF SUCCESS OFTEN LEADS US TO NEGLECT OUR PLAYFUL AND FEMININE NATURE.

Marriages can lose their spark, motherhood can become a never-ending to-do list, and demanding careers can push our sensuality into hibernation. Our playful, feminine side is often lulled into slumber, sometimes never to be awakened again.

I created The Feminine Connection to change that narrative. My purpose is to help women who want more out of life find a balance, so they experience both success *and* a luscious life, one filled with joy and their true feminine radiance. I'm proof that it is possible to live it all!

www.thefeminineconnection.com.au

LEAH POLWARTH

AUTHOR, TRAVEL CONSULTANT

It is a precious gift to experience a fairy tale kind of love. You know, the kind where a knight in shining armour sweeps you off your feet. That was my Steve. Sadly, our love was only meant to last for a couple of chapters in the book of my life.

I was approaching 30 and had not experienced any long-term, stable relationships. I wanted love, but I wasn't really looking for it 'cause I was so busy. The moment I took a step back from juggling fulltime work along with nights and weekends performing in my covers band, Steve was there.

Steve was an arborist and the lead singer in a heavy metal band and he saw me in a way I wanted to be seen. He was my biggest supporter and I know it sounds cliché, but I became a better person because of him.

My life became more of a fairy tale than I ever anticipated. It was legit like my whole life just fell into place. We had the wedding with the Cinderella dress, and a year later, just as we planned, I fell pregnant. Everything just seemed to flow so nicely because we were on the same page and when Billy came along, the parent chapter of our story began.

Just 10 months later, our world was ripped apart by the unimaginable – a stage four bowel cancer diagnosis. Steve fought as hard as he could, but after seven months, he was gone. It felt like the blink of an eye.

I held it together while Steve was with us, but once he was gone, my next chapters were full of grief and depression while trying to be there for Billy. I had to overcome self-doubt and self-sabotaging thoughts so I could believe in myself and my abilities. There have been many obstacles, but at the end of the day the biggest one is your mindset.

I BELIEVED I WAS STRONG. I PERSEVERED AND THAT'S HOW I WAS ABLE TO FIND CLARITY ON THE OTHER SIDE OF GRIEF.

Billy truly was my saving grace. I put a lot of pressure on myself to write and publish my book, *Letters to Billy,* while working my job in travel, adjusting to being a single mum, managing my grief and building our house. Once we have our forever home, a gift from Steve, and have etched our own groove within the community, I look forward to more carefree days. What inspires me right now, is the prospect of simplicity. It's time to enjoy life and reconnect with that funny, happy-go-lucky Leah of old.

More importantly, now that my story has been told, I can fully step outside of the hardest part of grief and no longer be defined by the labels that came out of my love story: widow, cancer carer, single mum.

Billy and I are moving on to the next chapter; me and him against the world. We are blessed that we've never been truly alone thanks to an incredibly supportive network of friends, family and even the wider community, who have done so much for us.

The fact that I'm here and able to start another chapter is a blessing every day and that's what I'm grateful for.

www.letterstobilly.blog

LISA CURRY

AO, MBE, OAM, 3 X OLYMPIC AND COMMONWEALTH GAMES SWIMMER, AWARD-WINNING BUSINESSWOMAN, INTERNATIONAL SPEAKER, AWARD-WINNING AUTHOR, SUPER GRANNIE

The soft swish of my oar against the water in the ocean off the Sunshine Coast is music to my ears. My focus narrows to the perfect 45-degree angle ahead and the next thrilling wave. I find so much joy in this simplicity and flow, the focus of this season of my life.

I was 'just Lisa' when legendary swim coach Harry Gallagher discovered me in a Brisbane pool at 10 years old. From the moment I competed in my first race I had an insatiable hunger to be the best.

AT THE AGE OF 12, I KNEW I WOULD NEVER SETTLE FOR MEDIOCRITY.

Without goals, you won't get out of bed at 5am each day with the intention to do your best, and I wanted to stand on the podium. In that season when swimming was my lifeblood, the world got to know every inch of Lisa Curry. I won national and international medals and represented Australia 16 times over a 23-year career. I am the only Australian swimmer to have held Commonwealth and Australian records in every stroke except backstroke.

At 22, I married ironman champion Grant Kenny. There was no money in swimming back then; I had to find ways to make a living from who I'd become and what I knew. Grant was business savvy and helped establish the next season of me: Lisa Curry-Kenny, one of Australia's first fitness entrepreneurs. I embraced motherhood, welcoming daughters Jaimi and Morgan even as I nurtured my ambitions. The audacious, impossible goal of making the '92 Barcelona Olympic team at the age of 30, was proved possible, even with the sleepless nights tending to small children. The media waited for me to fail, but I'd put in the work and stepped onto the starting blocks, confident and secure: the outcome no longer mattered. Those Games remain my professional highlight. Two years later, son Jett completed our family.

When Grant and I separated in 2009, I rediscovered my strength as an independent woman despite a serious health scare. Decades of numerous elite sports had so heavily tested my heart, I needed a defibrillator. I embarked on the remarkable One Life One Chance Aussie Road Trip in 2012, visiting 100 towns in my motorhome to raise awareness for heart disease prevention.

I've been inducted into sporting halls of fame and received awards for my business, Happy Healthy You, and my 2022 memoir *Lisa*. But those trophies and medals aren't on display in the house. While they are nice to have, they are temporary. Only memories and family are truly lasting.

While I have my husband Mark in my corner, the last three years have been soul-destroying. Menopause and being physically stagnant due to injuries were extremely difficult, but I was overcome with grief when I lost Jaimi to long term illness. I honour her by giving myself the time and space to grieve. Now, for the first time in my life I have no plans or big goals. There's nothing left to prove.

In a beautiful circle, I'm Lisa again. When I'm not working or on stage speaking, I'm a normal grannie of three, a daggy homebody getting on the mower, pottering in the garden or crocheting. I am a boho hippie at heart with a hat, flowers in my hair, and thongs on my feet. In this season, I just want to *be* Lisa and live life on my terms.

www.happyhealthyyou.com.au

LOU O'BRIEN

"If you dream it, you can do it."
- *Walt Disney*

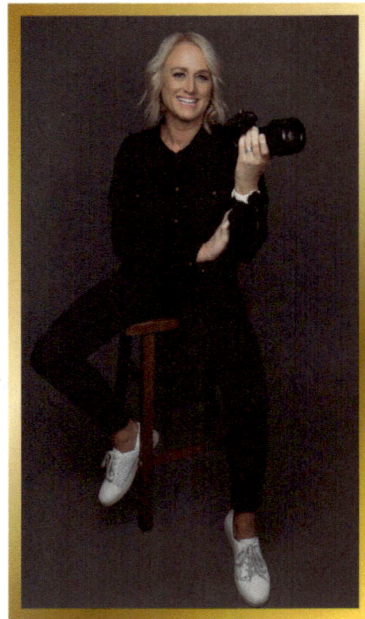

LORNA WILLIS

"If your attitude determines your altitude, can you imagine how high you could fly?"
- Lorna Willis

LISA WILSON

"Coming together is a beginning; keeping together is progress; working together is success."
- *Henry Ford*

LOUISE THOMPSON

"I stand on the sacrifices of a million women before me thinking what can I do to make this mountain taller so the women after me can see farther."
-     Rupi Kaur, Legacy

MARIA FAULDER

"Luxury lies not in opulence, but in the absence of vulgarity."
- Coco Chanel

MARIANGELA GAGLIARDO—MARSKELL

"Chi fa da sé, fa per tre." (He who works by himself does enough for three people.)
-     *Italian proverb*

LOU O'BRIEN

PHOTOGRAPHER SPECIALISING IN WEDDINGS

The day Mum allowed me to hold her Kodak Instamax film camera for the first time, I felt like the luckiest girl in the world. You had to have intention every time you pressed your finger on the shutter button, because each frame of film was precious.

I fell in love with photography when we practiced black and while film photography and wet processing for a semester at school. But I was told photography was a hobby, not a career, so I was advised to 'get a real job' and study primary school teaching instead.

Sitting in the university lecture theatre at the start of Semester Two, I wanted nothing more than to go to art college. When the professor announced, "You have until Thursday to tell administration if you want to continue or defer before your fees will be due," my hand immediately went in the air. "Where do I find administration?"

I had planned to build up a portfolio to apply for art college but came across a job listing for a 'darkroom technician' in the classifieds of the local newspaper. I knew in my gut this was my way into photography and my stepping stone was processing the shots taken by six press photographers each day in the newspaper darkroom.

It was a steep learning curve, but I began to see each photographer had a signature fingerprint in their work. I could identify who took which shot by examining the lighting, composition and angles they chose. I was so enraptured with my work that I never went to art college. I stepped out of the dark room, learned the art of photography on the job as a cadet press photographer and found my own fingerprint.

Creativity breeds creativity and as a lifelong learner, I love absorbing new techniques, so moving from film to mirrorless digital cameras has been a wonderful evolution.

YOU CAN SHOOT A MILLION PHOTOS IN A DAY NOW AND FOR MANY, THE PRACTICE OF CAPTURING MOMENTS IN TIME HAS LOST ITS POWER. NOT FOR ME. I STILL TREASURE EVERY SINGLE FRAME.

When I was made redundant from the paper 11 years ago, I couldn't imagine life without a camera in my hand and launched Images by Lou O'Brien within weeks with the support of my husband and twins. There was a period of adjustment as I began working from home and relying on myself to earn a living, but it was the best thing I could have done.

The reality is, I never feel like I 'work' because my craft brings joy to people every day as I capture memories they cherish for a lifetime. It takes a lot of hard work and determination to run a successful small business, but being driven by passion has stood me in good stead as an award-winning wedding and family photographer.

The awards have been nice, but my true joy comes from giving my clients a stress-free and fun experience so they are relaxed and natural. This creates timeless images. To capture history for people over the past thirty years has been an honour, especially in a career and business someone told me would never be a job!

www.imagesbylouobrien.com

LORNA WILLIS

INNOVATOR OF LOWANNA BEACH RESORT, WOW PROPERTY WOMEN AND THE PROPERTY EAGLES MENTORING ACADEMY

From very humble beginnings as a child being brought up in an old farm house, with no electricity or running hot water; with kerosine lanterns and an outside dunny; I could never have dreamed that one day I would be the developer of a beautiful 112 apartment complex known as Lowanna Beach Resort.

Though the desire to create versatile and useful spaces had always been there, even when I was fashionably designing and creating cubbies in hay stacks and treehouses when I was young, it wasn't until I was 30 years old and had my four beautiful daughters, that I knew what I wanted to be 'when I grew up'. My life had already begun to shift when we had an opportunity to build our first home from scratch. Seeing something come to life that had originated in my mind was a real WOW moment for me. That was when it all kind of clicked that I could really pursue property by qualifying as an Archtictural Designer.

From designer to developer was a natural transition. However it took a huge amount of faith to step out from the comforst zone of a weekly pay packet – and to back myself on project success alone! I have been blessed with some great results; from Australian Designer Awards to the most recent award, Winner Top 100 Women in Construction – Development Sector. Though the pinnicle will be the completion of the Lowanna Beach Resort.

But I have also had many challenges. One of the biggest of these and over the longest period, was pioneering in a male dominated industry to establish credibility and gain respect. Meanwhile there have been those sporadic challenges that I have survived; a motorbike accident; a car accident; a brush with suspected lung cancer; and having to rebuild my financial life at the age of 55 after a financial advisor embezzled from me.

CHARACTER BUILDING EXPERIENCES CAN HELP YOU TO BECOME THE PERSON YOU NEED TO BE - IF YOU LET THEM!

Having survived the trials and tribulations of decades of property cycles, my legacy now it to assist other women through the Property Eagles Academy; to overcome limiting beliefs and outdated predjudices; to rise to a whole new level of confidence and vigor that will enable them to conquer new horizons and build their own version of financial freedom, using property as the vehicle to get there. We also teach women how to protect themselves structurally!

For me personally, I think the secret to happiness is coming to peace with who you are and how you live your life. I feel joy every day I'm being grateful. Strange for some, but my meditation is riding my Honda 700cc motorbike. This forces me to focus and be in the moment. There's no room for error. But it is so freeing for the spirit and your senses come alive - you can smell everything as you ride along, from the scent of the lemon gums trees, to the cow patties in the paddocks!

For most women to really thrive, they just need likeminded sisters to help them tap into the awesomeness of who they are, to be encouraged and inspired in an environment that is supportive and protective. That's what we do!

www.wowpropertywomen.com.au

LISA WILSON

WISHLIST FUNDRAISING AND PARTNERSHIPS MANAGER

From the moment I joined Wishlist as one of a humble staff of three in 2006, I witnessed the ripple effect of better hospital treatment, support, equipment and training at the Sunshine Coast Health and Hospital Service that resulted from community donations. But it wasn't until my husband Scott and I welcomed twins Mali and Taj in 2012 that I experienced first-hand how vital our work is.

Taj was 18 months old when he was admitted to the Nambour Hospital ICU with meningitis and had to be intubated. I didn't know until he had recovered and I came back to work that he was the first baby to use the paediatric intubation equipment purchased through 92.7 Mix FM Give Me 5 For Kids.

It was such a full-circle moment! I first met Wishlist CEO Lisa Rowe when I came back from maternity leave specifically to manage the 2002 Give Me 5 campaign in my former marketing role at MixFM. Four years later, I had moved back in with my parents so they could look after my son Zac while I studied to become a primary school teacher. I was a single mum and just surviving financially with my eyes fixed on a brighter future when Lisa called to offer me the fulltime role at Wishlist.

I became a 'jack of all trades' learning everything on the run, with the focus of establishing the charity as a trusted entity on the Sunshine Coast. Asking businesses and residents to dip into their pockets is challenging, but we built relationships, showed up consistently and created several annual events that connected with different sections of the community.

IN OUR EFFORTS TO ACHIEVE GREATER SOCIAL GOOD, WE MUST WORK TOGETHER AND USE OUR INDIVIDUAL STRENGTHS TO ENSURE OUR OUTCOME IS SUCCESSFUL.

I am extremely proud of the Wishlist Spring Carnival, which I spearheaded 15 years ago after being inspired by a brainstorming session with lawyer and philanthropist Travis Schultz. It now raises close to $300,000 each year. An incredible $6.6 million has come from Give Me 5 and Wishlist has raised and directed more than $21 million over 25 years to the health service.

Due to our heavy reliance on event-based fundraising prior to Covid-19, Wishlist were faced with a potential loss of $750,000 once community health restrictions came into play in 2020. At the same time, our frontline staff were being stretched to the limit as more community members were accessing health services than ever before. It was time to innovate! I pitched an outside-the-box idea that wasn't welcomed with open arms at first, but I kept pushing. Through some of the best teamwork I have experienced, the digital fundraising campaign Wishlist Giving Day raised over $240,000 in just 12 hours and set the benchmark for fundraising in regional Queensland.

I am inspired every day by the Wishlist team, which has expanded to a paid staff of 27, but none of it would be possible without the unsung heroes in our community – the 120 Wishlist volunteers who have given tirelessly over the past 25 years and the people who continue to support our events.

Juggling motherhood, my fulltime career and running a household can be exhausting at times, but all I have to do is think of the lives we have saved and I am fired up, ready to continue succeeding.

www.wishlist.org.au

LOUISE THOMPSON

MANAGER OF VENUE 114 AND COMMUNITY SPACES, SUNSHINE COAST COUNCIL

B eing shy from a young age and loving to be by my beautiful Mum's side (something I still relish today!), it was exhilarating to finally find my voice through being courageous, kind and inclusive.

You could always count on me to stand up for anyone being bullied in the schoolyard.

I HAVE AN ENTRENCHED BELIEF THAT NOBODY IS BETTER THAN ANYONE ELSE AND YOU TREAT PEOPLE THE WAY YOU WOULD LIKE TO BE TREATED.

These values along with good manners, taking pride in your work, loyalty and laughing out loud lots has served me personally and professionally on my journey as a leader.

Commencing work in the events industry at 21, I have been fortunate to facilitate and create many wonderful experiences. Engaging with people, assisting to bring their celebration to fruition and exceeding my client's expectations is extremely rewarding to me.

This led to my second passion as a marriage celebrant at the age of 25. At the time, the average age of celebrants on the Sunshine Coast was 62! Meeting beautiful couples, hearing their love story and legally uniting them was a complete honour and delight. I absolutely loved this important role for 15 years until the unfortunate realms of Covid.

Acquiring the venue manager role at Venue 114 (formerly known as Lake Kawana Community Centre) by the age of 30 was a dream come true. Creating and activating a safe, welcoming, professional venue with event spaces for our community to celebrate, cultivate and immerse in, is amazing. Leading and empowering my team and watching them evolve and succeed brings me so much joy.

To recharge, I love nothing more than being at the beach with family, friends and watching the sunset over a champers. This, combined with exercising at sunrise overlooking the ocean, is the best way to start my day. It gives me time to think, breathe and be grateful for so much in my life. I then crank the tunes, put on my heels, a big smile and think to myself, *Go girl!*

My two beautiful children are what I am most proud of. They are best of friends, full of spunk, spirit and kindness and make my husband and I laugh every day. Although busy and a juggling act at times, they are a great reminder of what is most important in life, we cherish our time together as "Team Thomo" and I absolutely love being their mum.

As a leader, I am the change I want to see in this world! I have witnessed and experienced gender inequality and bullying which has further driven my compassion for, and need to welcome and celebrate diversity and inclusion. Creating positive, productive, cohesive, safe work environments for my team to flourish in is my ultimate priority. This is also reflected in my love for my community: when you align with your true passion and purpose and surround yourself with like-minded people, it's remarkable how many magical moments you can create.

I am courageous enough to stand up for what I believe in. I will lead with integrity, passion and purpose and encourage everyone, especially women, to shine bright as their true, authentic, stunning selves. Together, we can all leave an empowering positive footprint.

louise.thompson@sunshinecoast.qld.gov.au *www.venue114.com.au*

MARIA FAULDER

AWARD—WINNING OWNER, PASSIONATE COLOURIST AND STYLE DIRECTOR AT SUITE THREE

vividly remember the first time I experienced an inner knowing that everything was going to be alright. I was seven and probably too young to be wandering alone around Stanwix Bank in Carlisle, England. I was in awe of the beautiful, massive Georgian townhouses and peered through the windows as I went by, marvelling at the chandeliers and luxurious furniture, which were a far cry from the humble neighbourhood I lived in.

Despite how out of reach it all seemed, I felt a sense of excitement about what the future held.

I UNDERSTOOD THAT NO MATTER WHAT CAME ALONG, I WOULD BE ABLE TO OVERCOME IT.

That beautiful experience steeled me for the challenges life would bring.

My parents divorced when I was a teenager and although my mother had mental health challenges due to alcoholism and schizophrenia, I chose to live with her. I felt I had a duty to be there for her. But she delved deeper into her demons and although I know she loved me, I had to leave.

I spent school holidays with my dad at the art college where he taught fine art. He showed me how to develop prints, mix inks for silk screens and inspired me to appreciate colour, form and style. We'd go to London exhibitions and admire work by Andy Warhol and other greats. Growing up around a bunch of arty folk, I thought I'd end up at the art college, but when a friend started a hairdressing apprenticeship at 15, I thought *I kind of fancy that!*

I fell in love on Day One. I love the science of mixing colours, the balance of light and shade, contrast and depth. After 36 years, I can instantly make choices based upon a client's natural cool or warm colour universe.

I sold my first salon, Kudos, when I relocated from Carlisle to Buderim with my husband and eldest son in 2004. Before long, we welcomed another son and styling a small group of my best friends quickly grew into a large hair community. I thought, *you've got a business here girl, where are you going to put them all?* My craft is my currency, so I opened Suite Three in Buderim in 2008.

I'm not afraid to roll up my sleeves to take on something new. I've had a damn good man behind me since we were 18, and he bolsters my confidence to back myself, grow and develop. I've participated in 50 top runways for designers Alex Perry, Collette Dinnigan and Manning Cartel, the last five at New York Fashion Week. While fashion is thrilling, I thrive on connection with my clients. I use nonverbal cues to tell whether someone's style personality is classic, romantic or natural the moment they step through the door.

Juggling the business, raising our boys and being a carer for my husband while he awaited a kidney transplant were tough challenges, but we got through by focusing on the light at the end of the tunnel. In 2018, our prayers were answered.

I always knew I would have a successful life, I just never imagined it would be on the beautiful Sunshine Coast with a community built on love, respect, style and colour.

MARIANGELA GAGLIARDO–MARSKELL

ASSISTANT MANAGING DIRECTOR FOR MAR GRA AND MUMAGER' FOR INTERNATIONAL MODEL AURORA MARSKELL

Life experiences define who we are and for me it was the moving around when I was young. I went to eight schools over three continents and lived in so many homes I lost count. I had loved ones and friends I left behind each time, but there was always the one constant: my family. It is from them that I draw all my strength, determination and love.

My parents, Graziano (John) and Eufrasia taught us that blood is always thicker than water and if you want to achieve something as a family, you need to stick together. They showed us the courage to move away from security and start again, they taught us that hard work always pays off and that you can fight, argue, and sometimes hold a grudge but when push comes to shove, your family is always there.

It is with this tenacity and resilience that they built our family business, Mar Gra, from nothing and it is like our family baby... you never put the baby down and walk away!

MY TWO BROTHERS AND I SAY WE HAVE STONE RUNNING THROUGH OUR VEINS, NOT BLOOD!

Although my father is a little old school and didn't want me to have the hands on experience of creating beautiful stone finishes, he has always backed me as his right-hand in the office. I know my side of the business and the industry inside and out.

My brothers and I are equal managers in Mar Gra and more than three decades in, I still love the sector because the beauty of nature is at work, creating irreplaceable materials that never go out of fashion. To me, marble and Natural stone are the epitome of luxury. We do not deal in high-silica man-made products, so we create products that last forever, are environmentally friendly and now have served multiple generations of Coast families.

When I welcomed my daughter Aurora into the world 13 years ago, I split my dedication between nurturing the business and raising her to be a young woman that is as beautiful and good as she is intelligent and confident.

Aurora's passion is the fashion industry, and she has already walked international catwalks with the confidence of women twice her age. When I see her in her power on the runway, it is my greatest joy. Fashion and her modelling are our shared passion and a career that we are nurturing for Aurora; it also allows her to experience cultures, travel with us and keeps us together throughout.

Balancing my role as a managing director, 'mumager' for Aurora and a wife can be tiring, but I believe that if it was meant to be easy you wouldn't appreciate it as much; I have a beautiful life and to give them all my time is the least I can do. This is what makes me happy, and that is enough.

Through all of the highs and lows, it is a blessing to have spent my whole life with my family. For my husband and I to have been able to give Aurora that same beginning in life is the most important part. They say it takes a village to raise a child, in our case, I say it is the unconditional love of family that will raise our child to be a great woman one day because that courage and determination runs through all of our blood.

www.margra.com.au

MARY MARTIN

"We're all getting older, let's do it with gusto!"
- Mary Martin

MEERA ALLEN

"So speak as if the world entire were but a single ear, intent on hearing what you say; And so, in truth, it is."
- The Book of Mirdad

MORGAN GRUELL

"Be the woman who fixes another woman's crown without telling the world it was crooked."
- Leslie Littlejohn

NADIA COLBOURN

"Be yourself, everybody else is already taken."
- Oscar Wilde

NAN CAMERON

"When a great ship is in harbour and moored, it is safe, there can be no doubt. But that is not what great ships are built for."
- Clarissa Pinkola Estes

NATALIE BLACKLOCK

"People laugh at me because I am different; I laugh at people 'cause they are all the same."
- Vivekananda Swami

MARY MARTIN

HORMONE SPECIALIST, NATUROPATH AND CHIEF QUEEN OF HORMONE QUEENS

Ageing inspires me! It's not something you hear many women declare, but the reality is, we are all in this ageing process together. Once I support women to get on top of 'uninvited' symptoms of ageing and or peri/menopause, they can truly enjoy coming into their power at that stage of life. After all, we are older, wiser, more intuitive, and willing to put up with less bullshit, but that doesn't mean the fun and wonder of life has to stop!

I am a passionate advocate of changing up the conversations, attitudes, clichés and norms around the female ageing process. Working with women to help future proof themselves with natural, proactive tools so they enjoy a rewarding quality of life and longevity is my passion.

I was drawn to natural therapies at the age of 27 when I experienced unexplained chest pain. It baffled doctors, but a naturopath discovered I had gall stones. I remember thinking, *I don't even know what a naturopath is… but I want to be one!* I had already committed to a contract teaching English in Korea, but I took anatomy, physiology and biochem books with me. Those subjects scared the shit out of me, and I wanted to get across it all before I returned. This year I am so excited to be celebrating 20 years as a naturopath!

I had both of my children while studying naturopathy and because I focused on what I was putting into my body, I had *the* healthiest pregnancies. I literally became a 'hormone geek', wrote nine books and founded The Baby Builders to support couples overcome infertility and prepare for pregnancy.

Life doesn't always go to plan though, and heavy stuff has gone down in my life in the past seven years. After a prolonged period of personal trauma and grief, the emotional toll took up physical space in my body in the form of a neurological condition, turning my personal and professional life upside down. Through a lot of self-love, letting go and acceptance, I've come to terms with my new normal. Now I call it my superpower, because my life experiences can help others understand that we are not our 'conditions'.

I haven't done this alone, but have an inner circle of loved ones who keep me grounded, fill me with joy, pride, optimism, and gratitude. My amazing adult kids Quinn, Isla, Maddy, Tim and Lachy are my inspirations, my love, Charlie, is my human, and my 'Sistas' whom I am grateful to have: we lovingly have each other's backs and hearts.

I find that my curious nature fires up a childlike zest for life! I am in my element walking in the pouring rain, drifting on my paddleboard, watching birds and cloud formations and am a sunset freak: I'll stay right until the end of the glow! I have created Hormone Queens to help women harness their inner child, and to feel playful, happy, healthy and confident in our more 'mature years'! We are all such incredible, unique, inspiring women with beautiful hearts and minds who deserve to lead life to its fullest.

WE'RE ALL GETTING OLDER, LET'S DO IT WITH GUSTO!

www.hormonequeens.com

MEERA ALLEN

FOUNDER OF MANIFESTING DESTINY, YOGA TEACHER, SINGER, ARTIST, RADIO HOST, GRAPHIC DESIGNER

regularly ponder existence itself. That which was before time, before this earth, before this solar system, before this galaxy, before the infinite universe was ever even an idea - the vast and infinite nothingness from which we came and still are a part of.

Being South African born with Gujarati Indian heritage, I was raised in congruence with the Yogic philosophy and lifestyle. My parents had a strict discipline around meditation and even as a child we had regular conversations about death and the souls' karmic balance.

I obviously chose my parents as a foundation to catapult this knowledge even further, which includes a lifelong quest to live in brain, heart and body coherence, mainly through yoga. However, I've had three near-death experiences in my lifetime, but the first was the most transformational.

Through mosquitos I contracted Dengue Fever while in Salvador in 2002. I literally wasted away to skin and bone and had been lying in a hospital bed for days without the strength to even open my eyes. I could hear my fiancé's family around me when I felt a slipping sensation, like floating on a glassy ocean and you can't tell where your skin ends and the water begins. It was so peaceful and beautiful.

"Meera! Give us a sign. Are you going to live? Or are you going to die?" Vacuumed back into my body and pain gripped me once again, but my health began to improve. I had a sense of *you're not done yet, you've got some shit to do!* Feeling my soul exit through my crown chakra was the legit experience I needed to truly understand the theory of everything I had learned. It anchored me into my yoga practice and *ishvara pranidhana* – the joyful surrender to the divine grace. Every day I ask, "What is good for the agenda of my soul? Show me and I will follow that."

TRUSTING MY INTUITION AND LISTENING TO THE HIGHER DIVINE GUIDANCE HAS BEEN CRITICAL TO BELIEVE AND FULFILL MY MOST 'OUT THERE' DREAMS.

It has seen me re-invent myself over many careers from design to media, starting a capoeira academy to yoga, corporate to singing and art. Then there was the galactic musical theatre show I wrote, produced and performed in with a crew of 37 wonderful artists and musicians called Star Blue. Now my focus is on my business, Manifesting Destiny, and the Vocal Confidence course inspired by my mother, who went through so much suppression and struggled throughout her whole life to find her voice.

When you go to the primal, tribal part of every woman, we innately need to use our voice to communicate our soul song. When you have been suppressed, your throat chakra closes, you block the gateway between your heart and brain and you cannot tap into your true freedom of expression.

How can you know who you are if you cannot even find a safe place in your own body? Vocal confidence helps people to heal their trauma so they too can look externally at the moon and stars, reconnect internally to the infinite to follow their curiosity and creativity with reckless abandon. There's no need to hide any longer, speak up, speak impeccably, speak your truth proudly.

www.manifestingdestiny.com.au

MORGAN GRUELL

PERFORMER, DANCE INSTRUCTOR, FOUNDER OF MUM BUM

The glamour of feathers, heels, costumes and sparkles have played a huge role in my professional life, but the funny thing is, I was anything but graceful when I was a child. I loved to drag my hand along the road to get all dirty and gross, never wore shoes, climbed trees and my hair was a mess. But as I grew into a young woman, I was drawn to beautiful costumes and dazzling performance.

Growing up with Lisa Curry and Grant Kenny as parents, you would naturally think I'd be in the pool, where my sister Jaimi went, or in the surf, like my brother Jett. But I was always a little bit different.

I NEVER ASPIRED TO BE LIKE ANYONE ELSE; I'M ON MY OWN PATH AND ACHIEVED SUCCESS IN MY OWN WAY.

I spent my childhood as a competitive gymnast and tried my hand at sports aerobics, but I was able to transfer my strength, flexibility and coordination to pick up dance relatively quickly in high school. I devoured techniques for tap, ballet, musical theatre, hip hop and acro and even though I was average-to-poor at most things, I worked my butt off. I had my sights set on the Moulin Rouge in Paris, and dance became my sole focus six days a week.

Two years later, I had that dream job and loved everything about Moulin Rouge. The costumes, the choreography and dancing the can-can with the best in the world for two shows a night, six nights a week for 18 months: it was a dream. When I returned for another 12 months, I was proud to perform as a snake soloist. Finally I was swimming, but with four pythons!

When I returned home, I became a barre teacher and personal trainer, performing whenever I could. I made waves when I performed in Cabaret de Paris, an Australian production, while 15 weeks pregnant with my eldest son. I discovered a passion for samba and had my pregnant belly on display wearing my g-string bikini and big heels for Samba Tropicalia at 34 weeks with my youngest on board. It was a celebration of motherhood and pregnancy and I felt so powerful.

I've competed in Australasian Samba Queen every year since 2021. This year, I have also rallied a group of my Over 50s Samba students to shake it on stage. Their zest for samba is infectious and it just goes to show how dance really is for everyone, regardless of age or ability.

There are times when I feel like a circus performer, juggling balls that represent work, dance teacher, mum of three boys under five, wife and dancer. But it's so full on, it's as if the balls are on fire, I'm hopping from one foot to the other and checking my watch to see if we're running late… I am so blessed my husband Ryan and I have the support of our close families through all our ups and downs.

Losing my sister in 2020 was devastating. She was such a sentimental person with so much creative talent. I try to see and appreciate beauty in the small things in life, like Jaimi did. We were going to get matching tattoos on our wrists, but she chickened out! I now have a heart with a J in it so I can carry her with me always.

I dipped my toes into entrepreneurship when I launched Mum Bum, activewear for pregnant and nursing mothers, in 2022. I knew if I didn't take the leap, I would always wonder *what if*. Setting a goal and having the confidence to take the risk has served me well so far, and it's something I hope to instill in my boys as they find their own feet in the world.

Instagram @morgangruell

NADIA COLBOURN

SINGER/SONGWRITER

The thunder of applause from an audience anchored me to my craft, but it was in silence that I found true self-love and acceptance.

From the moment my friend Renée taught me the four chords to Tracy Chapman's *Talkin' 'Bout a Revolution*, I was hooked. I asked my parents for a guitar for my 13th birthday. My first original song poured out of me only days later and their gift was paramount to a successful musical journey and career.

Once that six-string was in my hands, I never let it go. I found such freedom of expression through music and as I got older, I became conscious of writing in a way that allowed any listener to connect and find their own meaning in my lyrics.

IT FELT INCREDIBLE TO GIVE AN EMOTIONAL EXPERIENCE OR OPPORTUNITY TO HEAL THROUGH MY SONGS.

I've tried my hand at hospitality, administration, tourism, media, education, photography and property management looking for a perfect fit professionally, but my soul comes alive when I perform.

I have played more than 500 shows at festivals, on cruise ships and alongside Kasey Chambers, Ross Wilson and The Black Sorrows. I toured with Wendy Matthews and made it to the Top 100 of Australian Idol in 2006. Five years later, the video for my single 'Shooting Star' was a finalist in the WA Country Music Awards.

Supporting Pete Murray at his Noosa show in 2015 was my last gig before spinal surgery put an abrupt stop to performing. It was soul-destroying: I'd finally started to make some tangible traction with my music career after years of hard work, and now I was literally at a standstill.

I focused on physically healing so I could claw my way back onto the stage, but I never expected to go through a spiritual awakening. I had previously bought books and crystals to find ways to 'fix' the self-doubt and feeling of not being good enough, which had grown over a lifetime of falling in love with the wrong boys and constantly seeking validation from men.

It wasn't until I was pulled into a world of silence – devoid of musical chords and applause – that I could truly slow down and hear a universal truth: I am enough and I am beautiful. This simple, yet incredibly powerful, realisation allowed me to break down the walls I had built over decades and embody self-acceptance and self-love. I have found my ultimate freedom because the beauty I see in others is the beauty I now see in myself.

You don't have to wait for something to happen to you in order to find that inner peace, you can access it right at this very moment, wherever you are. The answers are always within and if you slow down and become quiet, you will find them.

I am back on my feet, writing a new album and in my natural habitat on stage and it feels so uplifting. My newfound appreciation for the power of presence and quiet within has brought a whole new energy to my music and I cannot wait to inspire even more people with this second era of my career.

Facebook Nadia Colbourn Music
Spotify Nadia Colbourn

NAN CAMERON

MASTER OF COUNSELLING, REIKI MASTER, FOUNDER OF PLENTIFUL LIFE COUNSELLING

t is no accident that we are here on this earth. Every single one of us has something beautiful and special to contribute to the world, but so many of us do not see the gifts we carry. I know, because it took me decades to recognise the gifts I've had inside me all along.

I was born into a family that didn't want me. My autistic father would arrive home each day, tired and stressed from work, and have meltdowns with me as the target. Even as a toddler I remember cowering from the force of his rage and destructive words. I had no comfort from my mother or sister. My Scottish Pa was the one adult in my life I felt accepted me.

HE NURTURED MY UNDERSTANDING OF WHAT HE CALLED 'THE SECOND SIGHT,' A CONNECTION WITH SPIRIT AND HOW ENERGY FLOWS THROUGH EVERY LIVING THING.

I sought solace from a household that made me feel worthless by climbing a grand tree in our backyard and sitting in its gentle embrace for hours, moving as one with the sway of the branches in the wind.

When I became a wife, mother of four and a qualified nurse, we struggled through life in the Blue Mountains. Unable to develop meaningful friendships or integrate into a supportive community, we jumped at the opportunity to move to The Netherlands' 'Green Heart'. Cycling through the lush farmlands every day connected me with nature and I felt valued by the genuine connection to the ex-pat community. Finally, I was someone.

When we came back to Australia eight years later, I went back to being no one. My nursing registration had expired. I worked unfulfilling odd jobs. My health began to fail. The GFC hit, severely devaluing the house we'd bought in the Netherlands and hadn't been able to sell. I was so stressed: there was no time to ground myself, everything piled up and I spent a lot of time crying in bed, feeling like my family would be better off without me.

A lifeline was thrown my way when I responded to a SalvoCareLine ad and was challenged to consider what my dream job would be. I immediately knew: counsellor! I accessed FeeHelp to complete a Bachelor and Master of Counselling because I finally found a way to combine my analytical mind with my powerful second sight.

I felt a spiritual calling to move to the Sunshine Coast and there, I finally found home and that feeling of truly being valued. I rediscovered writing, poetry, painting, and hugging trees. I opened Plentiful Life Counselling in 2016 and help people rediscover their special gifts and acknowledge how inspiring their stories of survival are.

So many people feel the energy of the earth, but don't understand it. I introduce my clients to grounding and encourage them to engage with trees, to lean on them and feel their gentle energy and to see the waves as they rush to kiss their feet. I try to open their eyes to the magic of life and the healing of our connection to the earth and universe. Because when they truly know how much a part of this world they are, their unique gifts are free to shine, just as mine now do.

www.plentifullifecounselling.com.au

NATALIE BLACKLOCK

AWARD-WINNING FASHION DESIGNER, FOUNDER OF RAINBOW GODDESS AND BLACK DEVINE

"Natalie, if anyone ever asks you how you are, just say 'I'm good thanks,' because no-one actually cares, they're just being polite." This guidance when I was a child caused me decades of pain and suffering.

Over 23 years, my big smile and "I'm good thanks" hid the fact I never healed from the loss of my only daughter Aaliyah. I was so used to putting on a show like a clown and pretending everything was fine. I was in so much pain, yet on the outside I was the epitome of success, juggling a booming business and raising my three sons.

I MIGHT HAVE BAGGAGE, BUT HEY, AT LEAST IT'S DESIGNER!

I am a third generation designer and launched my first label in 2006 as an homage to Aaliyah, becoming the first Aboriginal fashion designer in history to showcase at New York Fashion Week in 2013. I won awards and was mentored by some of the biggest names in fashion, even being exclusively stocked in David Jones after turning down a massive offer from Target.

I had to bootstrap everything, but I felt so alive when I created. Seeing so much beauty in the vibrant colours and designs of Aboriginal and Torres Strait Islander artists, I established collaborations to print their paintings onto sustainable, high quality lycra made from regenerated plastic bottles and fish nets found in the Mediterranean ocean. My range has expanded to feature beautiful silks and kaftans and the stories of the artists are kept alive on the swing tags of flattering swimwear, lingerie and festival wear.

Professionally, I was smiling, but everything else was in tatters. In 2022 I gathered the strength to walk away from my marriage. I had nowhere to live and no car to drive. No longer the backbone of my family, I was suddenly and completely alone and felt so lost and depressed. A breast cancer diagnosis came four weeks later. I believe in metaphysical anatomy and was not surprised it started in my milk ducts, the very thing a mother needs to nourish her baby.

I am an Aboriginal descendant of the Ngarabal and Biripi people and my mother is Greek, so I drew inspiration from the goddess Athena during my breast removal surgery and chemo treatment. After all, my Greek ancestors cut off their breast to improve the aim of their bow and arrows and hit their target. This knowledge gave me the strength to get through my mastectomy: ain't nothing gonna get in my way! I now have Athena, complete with her mastectomy scar, tattooed in a half-sleeve on my right arm.

At 40, a friend assured me, "Nat, people do care, so start speaking up!" I feel empowered when I lighten my load and connect with my sisterhood to heal; no more "I'm good thanks". I have emerged as the Rainbow Goddess. It is not just a fashion label and the name of my Mooloolaba boutique, it is a way of being. It speaks to the Dreamtime's rainbow serpent and the Greek goddesses, but ultimately to my own survival of the storm. Now I see a rainbow every day – even if it is me wearing rainbow colours! Now, I am truly free and I'm gonna soar past that rainbow. Ain't nobody gonna stop me as I rebuild my life!

www.rainbowgoddess.com.au

NATALIE SINCLAIR

"What is meant for you won't pass you by."
- Nandini Chukka

PIPPA

SCOTT

"Whether you think you can, or you think you can't, you're right."
— Henry Ford

REBECCA

VIZI

"You are stronger than you think you are, never give up & listen to your body."
- Rebecca Vizi

RENEE PAOLINI

"My mission in life is not merely to survive but to thrive; and to do so with some passion, some compassion, some humour, and some style."
- Maya Angelou

RENEE VITELLI

"I hope to arrive at my death, late in-love and a little drunk."
- Atticus

ROBYN HILLS

"Bigger, bolder, brighter, better and more beautiful."
- Robyn Hills

NATALIE SINCLAIR

DIRECTOR AT SINCLAIR PROPERTY GROUP

Standing at the top of Alexandra Headlands staring out over Mooloolaba Beach, the source of many years of mind-clearing ocean therapy and inspiration for me, I was taking a mental snapshot of my life when a single thought stopped my mind in its tracks: *Is this how I want my life to look at forty?*

I was 38, we were in the middle of the 2020 Covid lockdowns and I was out for exercise – one of the few reasons why you could leave your home at the time. With just two years to go, I realised I wanted to make some *big* changes across the board. I was stuck in a rut… not that it was a *bad* rut, but I knew there was more out there for me.

I think when we become mothers, we can believe the falsehood that you forego the adventures of your twenties and exchange them for a life of responsibility and routine, that you can't make a change, adjust your sails and head off in a new and exciting direction.

I WAS READY TO TAKE A HUGE LEAP OUT OF MY COMFORT ZONE AND BE THE CAPTAIN OF MY OWN SHIP.

Even though I didn't yet know which direction to go, I decided then and there that I was going to change up my whole life. I have career leapt from publishing to e-commerce and now real estate. None of these changes were done at the 'right time' and none were calculated risks, each were sink or swim, succeed or fail moments.

Despite the fact I seem quite confident and always have a huge smile, I've suffered from anxiety my entire life: it's not always easy to pump up my tyres to take these bold leaps. But just seven weeks after my epiphany, I had a real estate license and quickly found it was the profession that had been waiting for me all along!

I have taken a lifetime of skills, knowledge and experience and poured them into real estate. I spent over 20 years in real estate marketing and publishing and won the 2012 Sunshine Coast Young Business Woman of The Year Award as Managing Director for the National Real Estate Magazine Coast to Coast Media, and in 2019 was awarded the title of Sunshine Coast Small Business Woman of the Year with Miss Monogram, a brand I founded and built from the ground up before selling in 2021.

I was awarded Ray White Premier status, which placed me in the top 10 per cent of Ray White agents nationally in my first year. Knowing my son and daughter watch how I show up in the world will always inspire me to show them how incredible your life can be if you commit to putting in the work.

In 2022, I ventured out as a principal with my partner in life and business, Mitch, to establish Sinclair Property Group. We provide a heart-led experience for our clients, acknowledging the fact that we go on an emotive journey with them. There are happy and sad tears, we hold people's hands and we celebrate or commiserate and I love that people trust us to share this with them.

Life is really what you make of it. I wake up every day grateful that I took the reins in 2020 and stepped boldly forward. It just goes to show that you can chase a new horizon, no matter what age you are.

www.teamsinclair.com.au

PHILIPPA SCOTT

THE RICHARDS TRAUMA PROCESS PRACTITIONER, PERINATAL MENTAL HEALTH AND PARENTING SUPPORT SPECIALIST

Cradling my firstborn and staring into her eyes, I forgot about the induction and emergency caesarean I'd just been through to bring her into the world. I pushed my physical discomfort to the side to focus on how to do this 'mum thing'.

Once my daughter was three months old, I could finally think about my birthing experience. This was my *first step on a long journey, one which acknowledged the role and effects of trauma in birth and parenting.* While looking through resources from the Maternity Coalition and the Homebirth Movement, I became angry; induction leads to a high risk of emergency caesarean births and nobody had told me that. I'd had what I like to call an 'unne-caesarean'.

I couldn't let others suffer as I had: I needed to be that support person for other women and became a doula and childbirth educator, launching Birth Buddies in 2004. My belief and passion for advocating and supporting women and families around the time of birth is so strong, I worked my heart out and established the Townsville Birth Centre. I was president from its inception and first few years in operation. I'm proud that it still runs today, providing thousands of families with family-centred midwifery care in a fabulous environment.

I had three more daughters with incredible births, but as they grew, I felt like I was parenting from guilt and overwhelm. When my third daughter was diagnosed as being on the Autism spectrum, I fell into adrenal fatigue.

I would fall asleep on the couch at 7.30 at night, leave food on the bench, take wrong turns while driving to work... I was physically crumbling from being in constant flight or fight mode: there was absolutely no time to freeze!

I laughed at the GP when he said I needed three months off and thought a change of career was a better option. I found an ad that described me perfectly; working for a trauma training company that created The Richards Trauma Process. I devoured the content and within 15 days, my life changed completely. I realised that while I hadn't experienced any majorly traumatic event, many heavily stressful periods had affected my way of being.

Yet again, I knew in my heart that I needed to help others. Now, I give my undivided focus to my business, Fantastic Futures, empowering new and expectant parents to build strong and healthy relationships with their children and create fantastic futures for their families.

IT'S WONDERFUL TO SEE MORE PEOPLE TRYING TO CONSCIOUSLY PARENT, BUT I FOCUS ON THE SUBCONSCIOUS, BECAUSE THAT IS OPERATING 90–95 PER CENT OF THE DAY.

Just as I had experienced, many parents have a subconscious fight, flight or freeze response in constant operation: it can happen even if there isn't a clear trauma catalyst.

If we can resolve this at a cellular level, instead of parenting from reactive instinct (a fancy term for fear), you can tap into intuition, a place of love and deep knowing.

If we really want to change the world into a more loving place, we need parents who can operate out of love, not fear. Changing the future generation begins with how we show up as parents, and I'm so thankful my experiences have shown me how.

www.fantasticfuture.com.au

REBECCA VIZI

ALL-ROUND #PINKSPIRATION, DISABLED BODYBUILDER ATHLETE

The music was pumping as I stood backstage at the 2023 ICN Queensland bodybuilding competition. The moment I heard the crowd cheer, I was in the zone.

The women about to walk on stage alongside me in the Sports Model First Timer Category were wearing baby blue ICN sports bras and black bikini bottoms with a baby blue band. Those outfits just didn't feel like me, and weeks earlier I'd approached one of the judges at a posing class to make a special request... I wanted to wear pink.

Pink lifts my mood and makes me happy, so I surround myself with it. With my pink hair, outfit and my silver and pink cane in hand, I would embody #pinkspiration on stage.

I WAS READY TO STAND TALL AND SHOW THAT WHEN YOU HAVE A DISABILITY OR HAVE MENTAL HEALTH CHALLENGES, FIND SOMETHING YOU LOVE AND NEVER GIVE UP, THINGS WILL GET BETTER.

Less than two years earlier, I had undergone two hip surgeries to repair a labral tear, was diagnosed with Functional Neurological Disorder (FND) and had been told I was going into early menopause. I was only thirty three.

It was a battle for me to get the FND diagnosis . Medical professionals thought the symptoms I was experiencing were all in my head. But I kept pushing and after I experienced 'drop foot' - a condition where your foot goes limp – extensive testing finally found the cause.

For many years, I had also dealt with Borderline Personality Disorder (BPD) and felt like I was in the darkness, unseen and definitely misunderstood. There were times when overwhelming frustration or sadness would keep me down for months at a time.

I nurtured my mental health and overcame BPD through my faith and eight years of soul-lifting Zumba classes at Fernwood. Thankfully, at the time of the FND diagnosis my mental health had never been better, and I am so grateful for that.

FND has presented me with some unique challenges: my brain has trouble connecting with my lower body and left arm. I had to rely on a walker before graduating to a walking stick. Once I felt steadier on my feet, I went back to the gym. I did Zumba classes sitting on my walker until I was strong enough to stand. I started strength training with the assistance of my exercise physiologist and physiotherapist Hayley Wilkinson and got some much-needed tough love from Olympian Lisa Curry, who I connected with while in hospital.

I then met body building champion Leon Stensholm through my mum's church and asked if I could train with him. I felt in my gut that I needed a goal; I had gone so long without something to focus on. Leon agreed to help prepare me to compete in the ICN.

The atmosphere at the competition was electric as I stepped out onto the stage. I felt on top of the world as a large gold medal was placed around my neck: I won the Physically Challenged category!

I still experience tingling and other FND symptoms, but Commonwealth Games para-powerlifter Hani Watson is mentoring me to take my physical abilities to the next level.

Step by step, I'm making new goals and reaching my dreams.

@pinkspirationbec on Instagram or Rebecca Vizi on Facebook.

RENÉE PAOLINI

CEO EASTHOPE EVENTS, CO-FOUNDER OF HEAD SPACE LIVE

I recently found out that I am a Projector and I'd never truly appreciated this Human Design label until I realised it speaks to the core of who I am. It explains why I am a leader, an organiser, a connector and have the wisdom to guide others in the most efficient ways to use their energies, gifts and talents.

As a young woman, I didn't know who I truly was other than I had a strong sense of adventure and self-belief. I travelled the world as a cabin supervisor for Virgin Blue Airlines for seven years and moved from the air to the ocean, working on private luxury yachts.

Those years were thrilling, but life was surface level. It was all about fancy dinners, serving billionaires and royalty, minimal responsibility and working to be able to pay for the next *thing*... a house, a wedding, a new car.

My journey of self-discovery and awakening began when I welcomed Arley May to the world in 2016, followed by Lennox Rose two years later.

My beautiful babies provided me with the inspiration and drive to do life on our terms, with compassion and integrity, and to stand up for who and what I believe in: to dance, laugh, create, collaborate and experience all the emotions and challenges that make up the human experience.

I found professional passion in events management and worked in various businesses. Yet in 2021, I became one of the many people around the world terminated from jobs they loved because of their health choices. I vowed to never have a boss again.

The reality is the world feels like it's having a massive awakening shift and old paradigms are crumbling for the good of all. It is an energy that has empowered me to step out as my weird, wonderful, authentic self and embrace the two very different sides of me; I love grounding in the garden with my chickens but I also love getting all frocked up and socialising.

In 2022 I launched Easthope Events to help other people shine authentically through unforgettable and timeless luxe events. I love being the hype girl, to bring guests together and spotlight people who are in their genius zone while I am in mine.

I also nurtured my craving to have deeper conversations and connect with the conscious business community by launching Head Space Live, an event series, with my business partner Judy King in 2023.
By stepping into my Projector type, I have been able to harness my talents while giving less f***s about what people think of me.

I CAN LEAD WITH HEART AND STRENGTH, KNOWING THE PEOPLE WHO ARE MEANT TO BE IN MY LIFE WILL MAKE THE EFFORT TO WALK ALONGSIDE ME.

This life is short and I am determined not to be a 90-year-old woman with regrets she didn't live her best life. So be bold, say yes to stuff even when it freaks you out. See, smell, taste and touch the world. Travel and experience new cultures. Don't play small. Try to make the world a better place in your own little pocket, because it all adds up to a legacy our next generation can be proud of.

www.easthopeevents.com.au

RENEÉ VITELLI

BUSINESS ANALYST, DONATE LIFE ADVOCATE

My greatest hero is someone I never met, but they gave me the ultimate gift: a second chance at life. In 2015 my lungs were failing after a lifetime of the physical stress of Cystic Fibrosis (CF). Coming face to face with your own mortality is confronting for most 25-year-olds, but then my parents had been told I would not likely survive past two, then five, then 10... there was always a number hanging over us.

My parents were regimented with my health care, so I didn't feel the full effects of CF until the teenage years. I thought I was 10-feet tall, bulletproof and the doctors didn't know what they were talking about, so I stopped taking medication. It backfired and I spent every school holidays in hospital throughout Years 11 and 12.

I DIDN'T WANT TO BE THE 'SICK KID' BECAUSE THERE WAS SO MUCH PITY ATTACHED, SO I BECAME DRIVEN TO SUCCEED AND BUST PEOPLE'S PERCEPTIONS OF MY LIMITATIONS.

I powered through a Bachelor of Business and Tourism scholarship at the University of the Sunshine Coast (USC) while working and studying full time, however, my health began to progressively decline after graduation.

I was forced to stop work when I was 25: my life had become a cycle of being in and out of hospital. My quality of life diminished. I needed a non-invasive ventilator to oxygenate me so I could sleep properly and spent 20 hours at a stretch in bed. I struggled to eat because pressure on my diaphragm made me vomit. I didn't have the space to breathe with a full tummy.

A double lung transplant was the only way I could survive. Transplants are not granted on a most deserving or first-come, first-served basis. There is genetic compatibility and other requirements to ensure the organ has the best possible chance of survival. I did the best I could to make myself an ideal recipient.

The estimated wait time was between five to eight months, but I didn't have that long. Miraculously three months later, I walked up to the reception desk at Prince Charles Hospital at 9pm and said, "My name's Reneé, I'm here for a double lung transplant," like I'd just ordered a cheeseburger from the Maccas drive through. It felt surreal, I kept thinking I would have to go back home, that it wasn't meant to be so easy.

I recovered physically in record time, walking around the ward within 16 hours and was home in 10 days with new lifelong medications. That's when the mental recovery began. I didn't plan for this part of life, so it was both humbling and challenging to look back on the person I was and decide who I wanted to be moving forward.

With a strong body and mind, the work ethic I cultivated as a young student has seen me flourish in my career. The scar on my chest is a physical reminder of my fight for life and I am determined to continue to make people aware of **how damaging perceptions can be. You never really know the strength that lies inside another person.**

One organ donor can save the lives of up to seven people! Souls go to heaven, organs don't: please talk with your next of kin and make your intentions known on the Donate Life registry today .

https://www.linkedin.com/in/renee-vitelli-809227143/

www.donatelife.gov.au

ROBYN HILLS

AWARD–WINNING PHOTOGRAPHER, ARTIST, FASHION DESIGNER, PROPERTY DEVELOPER, HELICOPTER PILOT

've given myself the new middle name of 'Tenacity,' because I didn't particularly like the one I was given. Every time I was told I couldn't do something, I just went ahead and did it.

IT TAKES TIME, COMMITMENT, ENERGY AND SOMETIMES NOT MUCH SLEEP, BUT I'D RATHER WEAR OUT, THAN RUST OUT!

I got stuck into anything creative I could do with my hands, painting, drawing, sculpting and even designing clothes at 12 years old, but when I joined a camera club at 16, I fell in love with the instant art of photography. I knew I could earn a living out of it, but was told: "You are a girl, we will not give you a job." I have now been awarded Master of Photography, been inducted as a Fellow of the Australian Institute of Professional Photography and won Australian Professional Photographer of the Year.

When I wanted to open my first photography studio, I was told by a business mentor that in order to have the greatest chance of success, I needed to be male, married with two children, 35 years old, have $20,000 capital, 10 years' experience and a desire to succeed.

I was a woman, single, 19, had $10,000 and no experience, *but* I definitely had the desire to succeed. I ran with that and a landlord in Nambour gave me a go. It didn't take long for me to catapult my business and at 22 years of age, bought my first Porsche and purchased my first investment property of four flats. See? Tenacity. I've got bucketloads of the stuff!

Even after 40 years, I am still underestimated at times and treated like I don't know what I'm talking about. It's fun having a gender-neutral name and seeing reactions when a male is expected to walk in the door, especially in the construction and development industry. When learning to fly at 38, the male testing officer quipped, "If girls were meant to fly, then the sky would be pink." I am now a qualified helicopter pilot and it has added a whole new dimension to my landscape photography.

My work has always been about people, though. I like to get inside my clients' heads and find out what they want to say to the world and how we can capture that in their portraits for an artistic interpretation.

I am grateful that my work has taken me around the world to follow what I call the 'Dots of Life': everything is connected. Taking action on one thing leads to something else; a landscape exhibition in New York led to the creation of a fashion label, and winning a photographic trip to Antarctica led to meeting my second husband.

I have a constant movie going on inside my head and it never stops, even at night I dream prolifically. To manage that, I make sure that I take some time out at the end of a project, to top up my energy and creativity. I've always had a curious mind, so when I'm challenged, I make a list of actions and ask *lots* of questions of people who have done it before. I'll never die wondering, I give most things a go, at least once, to see if I like it.

Tenacity has got me through it all.

www.ROBYNgraphs.com.au

ROCHELLE CALLARD

"You don't have to see the whole staircase, just take the first step."
- Martin Luther King Jr

SUZAN PRIOR

"What we spend our time and money on is what we value most."
- Russell Sterguss

TANYA BELL

"Be who you are and say what you feel, because those who mind don't matter and those who matter don't mind."
- Anonymous

TRACEY MORRIS

"Nothing is more important than empathy for another human being's suffering. Nothing. Not a career, not wealth, not intelligence, certainly not status. We have to feel for one another if we're going to survive with dignity."
- Audrey Hepburn

VERONICA WAIN

"You cannot do kindness too soon, for you never know how soon it will be too late."
-    Ralph Waldo Emerson

VIRGINIA ROBIN

"There is nothing either good or bad, but thinking makes it so."
-    Shakespeare's Hamlet.

ROCHELLE CALLARD

OWNER NUMBERWORKS'NWORDS SIPPY DOWNS

As much as you try to map out the path you want to follow in life, there are so many factors at play that you never really know what is around the corner. I had just welcomed my son Harrison and two weeks later, unexpectedly found myself a single mother.

Although I was overwhelmed at first, I knew in my heart I would do everything I could to provide my son with the opportunities he needed so he could have the most choices in life. That meant finding my independence and resilience and while it was challenging to find my feet at first, personal development became my beacon.

Every year since 1999, without fail, I have attended three Women's Circles. Being surrounded by powerful women has not only forged unbreakable bonds but has allowed me to consciously develop trust in my instincts and intuition so I could take calculated risks to plan for the future.

LIFE IS ABOUT OVERCOMING FEAR AND BELIEVING THAT YOU CAN DO SOMETHING, EVEN WHEN THAT LITTLE VOICE (AND SOMETIMES THE VOICES OF OTHERS) TELLS YOU THAT YOU CAN'T.

Intuition led me to a degree in education when Harrison was one and establishing a successful manufacturing and import business when he was eight. By being a strong and unwavering support in his life, he is now a 25-year-old law student at Monash University with absolutely no limiting beliefs, which I am so proud of.

In education, I found a drive to empower all children and help them to experience success. Like any human being, experiencing success in any capacity allows you to develop confidence and self-belief that you can take into all areas of life. When I became a principal for a small school in rural Queensland, I was able to establish a connected and respectful school culture that supported the whole community.

Everyone told me I was crazy to leave my secure Department of Education role to open the first NumberWorks'nWords on the Sunshine Coast, but I was 100 per cent confident. I *knew* this was the next step for me. There's nothing more satisfying for me than seeing that look of clarity in a child's eyes, that lightbulb moment when they finally experience success at something that has eluded them in the classroom.

It is a passion that is shared by every one of the 26 staff who work at NumberWorks'nWords Sippy Downs. I opened in January 2019 with zero students and we are now one of the top Queensland franchises, in the top 10 franchises in Australia and conduct 350 tutoring sessions a week.

I've become older and wiser, but I never believe I know everything. I'm always in a state of active growth, reflection and learning. I achieved a major health milestone in 2022 when I lost a lot of weight in nine months by hiring a coach and eating one plant based meal a day.

I was amazed at my resilience and still can't believe I did it. It showed me I can do anything I put my mind to and I strive to impart that to my students and staff. **As I've taken intuitive action, the next step in the staircase of life has appeared and now everything is manifesting in beautiful ways.**

www.numberworksnwords.com/au/our-locations/australia/sippy-downs/

SUZAN PRIOR

HEART MUM, NURSE AND FOUNDER OF SOUL2HEART

My grandfather learned the art of torture as an army sniper, a skill he passed down to his kids, who then used them on me. My parents didn't want me or my four siblings, so I was bashed, raped and burned as a child. I had to beg for anything I needed.

I ran away at 14 and found physical freedom, but it would take me many years to find freedom in my heart and soul. I've spent most of my adult life consciously making steps forward to overcome my trauma, find my voice and create a completely different life for my husband and daughters Emily and Tegan.

Tegan was born with heart, lung and kidney disease, five spleens, her stomach on the wrong side of her body and a double left lung, none of which were picked up during routine pregnancy scans. So much of my growth came from watching Tegan battle every day, being so hopeless and yet still fighting. In many ways, I felt like I was hopeless and still fighting too.

Being a 'heart mum' is never an easy feat, but as I became a powerful voice for Tegan, I learned how to advocate for myself too. I stood in front of the Health Rights Commission and demanded change to waiting times for children in emergency departments, as well as rights for pregnant women to have extra scans if they had concerns about their unborn babies. I won both of battles.

Having missed so much school, I had the literacy level of a Year 5 student, so when my husband encouraged me to apply for a hospital job in 2003, I went in ready to share all the reasons why I couldn't do it. But they accepted me with open arms and I began a career that has seen me plan hospital menus, cook and clean, work in aged care, assist in the medical ward as a qualified nurse and now work in the birth suite.

I haven't always felt strong enough to overcome the challenges life throws my way. I was driving with Tegan when we were hit by a truck in 2013 and our car burst into flames. Tegan was in ICU for three days and I was left with a bulging C2 and C3 disc that made any movement painful for months. Around the same time, doctors told me there was nothing more they could do to help Tegan's ongoing health issues. I dipped so low into depression that I considered taking my own life. Without knowing the depth of my despair, a female colleague reached out and literally saved my life.

When I look back over my life, I realise everything slotted in where it needed to perfectly. I offered so much resistance to each challenge, that I finally gave up… and that's when I let go of my need to control. Once that happened, magic followed and it actually made me grow!

I HAVE LOTS OF GIFTS IN MY LIFE BUT I DIDN'T FIND THEM UNTIL I FOUND MYSELF.

I have spent many years working to heal my trauma and had tried so many things that didn't work, so I'm determined to be a source of hope for other people by showing them what *did* work for me. I created Soul2Heart so other women can find their passion and purpose. It's a mission that inspires and empowers me every day.

www.soul2heart.com.au

DR TANYA BELL

EPIDEMIOLOGIST, CEO AND THOUGHT LEADER

The dedication note on my Public Health PhD thesis reads, "To my two periods of interruption." It is a term the academic world assigns to delays caused by things like chronic illness, a cancer diagnosis... or giving birth to children.

I was told I should "quit and become a housewife" when I fell pregnant in my first and last year of PhD through a National Health and Medical Research Council scholarship at Queensland Institute of Medical Research. But I had fought tooth and nail to cut a unique pathway to become an epidemiologist, so there was no way I was giving up. With my genetic predisposition, coupled with a rural upbringing, I thrive on persistence and completing everything I set out to do.

I had fallen in love with the medical field while studying communicable diseases in the second year of my science degree. The accepted route was to become a qualified general practitioner before specialising, but I wanted to cut out the middleman. I completed my honours and then contacted every university professor and research institute I could to catch a break.

Even though I was excited to be unexpectedly starting a family, I took a six-week "period of interruption" to give birth to my daughter before returning to fulltime PhD study so I didn't lose my scholarship. We couldn't afford childcare, so my husband became a stay at home dad and we lived off my $30,000 a year stipend. When I fell pregnant with my son, it would have been so much easier to just give up, but I finished the final copy of my thesis whilst nursing a one-week-old.

My unique opportunity was not lost on me. Whenever I felt like throwing in the towel, I thought of the next country girl with a big vision who might be turned away because the chance they took on me didn't pan out.

BREAKING OUT OF MOLDS IS REALLY HARD IN SOCIETY AND I WANTED TO PAVE THE WAY, NOT BUILD MORE HURDLES, FOR THE WOMEN WHO CAME AFTER ME.

As my career has evolved, I have taken roles where I could use my open mind, bravery, curiosity and drive for change in a way that can help vulnerable people have a better shot at the life a lot of us are really privileged to have. I was extremely tempted to dip back into epidemiology during the rise of covid, but my first priority as a leader was making sure everyone was safe. While I got my fix by having the John Hopkins data feed up on my computer, I had a risk minimisation plan and policies for staff and clients drawn up in record time to ensure vital services continued for vulnerable people.

I am definitely an "I can do it" person, even if I may not entirely know how to when I first lean into a challenge. Surrounding myself with quality mentors and positive people always helps! But being a short, blonde and (at one point) young female, I was often overlooked and underestimated throughout my career as an academic, lecturer and senior manager in public and private organisations and non-government agencies. I'm resilient though, and this underestimation is used as a big motivator to prove to myself and others that I can do anything I put my mind to.

https://www.linkedin.com/in/drtanyabell/

TRACEY MORRIS

CO-FOUNDER OF NO MORE FAKE SMILES

t's every mother's worst fear that something will happen to their child. I consider myself a fierce protector and had done everything in my power to ensure my four children were equipped for life, but I underestimated the power of a predator.

In our case, it came from the most unexpected source: the man I had been married to for ten years, the stepfather to my three eldest children and father to my youngest.

My world came crashing down in 2015 when my eldest daughter Annie made a comment in the heat of an argument about the man who was supposed to be her protector. I didn't hesitate. I believed her.

With the small amount of information I had, I knew I had to protect my children. I kicked my husband out of the house the next day and when Annie decided to make a formal statement and start legal proceedings, I was with her every step of the way.

It took three heartbreaking, anger-inducing, frustration-building years, but I worked my arse off to learn everything I could about the judicial process. I needed to understand Annie's rights and empower her to understand the decisions she had to make. Knowledge meant I could push back when the defence played dirty. The perpetrator received a sentence of 17 years and will remain behind bars for at least 11.5.

PEOPLE THINK ONCE A VERDICT IS HANDED DOWN, EVERYTHING IS SETTLED AND LIFE GOES ON, BUT IN REALITY, IT SIGNALS THE START OF ANOTHER EVEN MORE GRUELLING JOURNEY - ONE OF HEALING.

It has taken many years for us to process what happened and begin to heal. It isn't easy to come to terms with a disclosure. I have had my moments of rocking in a corner, not knowing what would become of my life, my family and our future. I wrote about this journey in my book, *I Believe You*.

But now put yourself in the shoes of that young person who comes to you and discloses they have been touched inappropriately by an adult. How could any decent adult ever expect that child to walk that path alone? It is our job to protect our kids, to hear what they have to say. Whether it is uncomfortable for us to hear or not, it is a thousand times more uncomfortable for them to endure.

In 2019, Annie and I stepped out as the co-founders of no more fake smiles, a nationally-recognised charity that creates a safe space where hope can live for child victims of sexual abuse. We provide grassroots support to victims and their families as an official Queensland Police Referral service for the greater Brisbane area. We advocate for nationwide systemic improvements to the judicial system, including through our recent participation in the #justiceshouldnthurt campaign spearheaded by journalist Nina Funnell, and also connect people to their therapy of choice so they can begin to heal.

no more fake smiles is committed to making positive change for our young people, but we cannot do it alone. I ask all adults to take responsibility. If a child speaks out, listen to them. If a child speaks out, believe them. If a child speaks out, respect them. If a child speaks out, above all else, support them.

www.nomorefakesmiles.com.au

DR VERONICA WAIN

ACADEMIC, FILMMAKER, PRODUCER, WRITER, DIRECTOR

The words inclusion and diversity were lofty ideals when my third child Allycia was born. Allycia's subsequent diagnosis of a deletion located on her 18th chromosome presented many challenges for her with fluctuating health. In many ways, she redefined our family and how we see the world.

I'd bumbled around as a young woman, having had some 50 or so jobs. The first was packing groceries at Woolworths. It took me a long time to embrace being an intelligent, forward-thinking woman. In my natural state I'm a hundred miles an hour, I get distracted easily and I'm impatient with myself.

I'VE LEARNED UNLESS YOU ANSWER THE CALL TO BE PRESENT, YOU ARE NOT GOING TO ACHIEVE WHAT YOU WANT TO.

Inspired by Allycia and the low expectations that accompany genetic difference, I've dedicated the past 28 years to finding ways to give people with disabilities the tools and agency to speak for themselves. Stories told on screen are a powerful medium, and have the capacity to reach audiences, and change hearts and minds like no other.

I'd always had a passion for film and when Allycia was three, I took on one subject a semester to complete a Media and Communication degree. I was a mature aged student when I created my first documentary, *The Creek*, which we sold to SBS. I explored narrative film and all three of my children featured in a barn dance scene in *Shorn,* a short that screened at the Hollywood Film Festival in 2007.

I found my niche in marrying creativity and advocacy with screen production and spent six years completing my PhD in Disability and Media Representation at Griffith Film School. But the way the industry was structured made it challenging to forge a fulltime career as a sole parent. I stepped back in 2009 and took a big leap of faith to move Allycia and I to Maleny. Here, we discovered The Sunshine Troupe, a performing arts group for people with disability and I became a founding committee member.

We flourished and created many original theatre productions together over 14 years. It was with a heavy heart that I chose to step away from my role as Producer and President in 2023. Fascinatingly, I realised the longest I'd ever stayed in one position was a voluntary role. It is a true reflection of my primary drivers: creativity and seeing people evolve and blossom as they find their own feet and voice.

I served on several boards over many years, including Vice Chair of Inclusion Australia, Parent to Parent, The Chromosome 18 Registry and Research Society. The work at this level is rewarding, but I found it challenging in terms of the anger and frustration I experienced as we continuously grappled with the slow rate of societal change. Nevertheless, I contribute to our family and our community where I can and am looking forward to presenting a paper on disability and inclusive filmmaking at the upcoming Visible Evidence Conference at the University of Udine in Italy.

I am now working with inclusive filmmakers Bus Stop Films and am a sessional academic with the University of the Sunshine Coast School of Law and Griffith University Film School. I think I have softened somewhat in my approach and am looking forward to seeing how we can influence change with love, kindness and empathy.

veronica_wain@yahoo.com.au

VIRGINIA ROBIN

PEACE CONSULTANT AND MEDIATOR AT CONSCIOUS BUSINESS CONSULTING GROUP, AUTHOR, TEDX SPEAKER

How ironic that I had to fall to my knees on a busy Mornington Peninsula street to see the world in a radically different way. There I was, world at my feet, successful partner of a law practice, strutting down Main Street wearing my favourite leopard print heels when I stepped out to cross the road and tripped over.

On hands and knees, the most embarrassed I'd been in my whole life, I wished the pedestrian crossing stripes would open up and swallow me whole. Alas, a guy got out of his car and scooped me off the road instead. My chiropractor prescribed yoga. It sounded like a punishment: I was more of a fast-paced Zumba girl, living on the edge. To me, yoga was akin to watching paint dry.

I went along begrudgingly, but after the first session, I felt *really* good. *There's something in this,* I thought as I went home determined to find out what 'it' was. Of course, my high achiever lawyer brain wasn't content with simply going to more classes. I began a 12-month diploma in yoga teaching in 2012 that opened a portal to a whole new way of being, one where the energy from which you make decisions plays a huge role in the outcome.

Choices made from a lower state of consciousness, like fear, will bring you negative experiences, while those made from a higher state of consciousness will have positive outcomes. It sounds woo-woo, but it's physics; literal science. My latest book, *Not guilty: Finding peace in three simple steps,* focuses on these principles.

WE ARE ALL ENERGY WHERE YOUR WORLD REFLECTS YOUR STATE OF BEING.

Combine that with the understanding that life is the sum of the choices we make and you can see how it works. This turned my world upside down, and lawyering didn't make sense anymore. I saw our legal system as a fear-based model designed to outsource blame. We want *them* to change. There really are no winners. Ultimately, I chose to leave my profession.

I learned firsthand how my state of being created my reality. I left a discordant marriage of 30 years, twice. The first time, I left in fear for my safety. I returned after promises of change but only the externals did and the old patterns soon re-emerged. So I embodied the feeling of being in a state of paradise.

When I moved to the Sunshine Coast in 2020, that is exactly what my life became: living by the beach, creating art. I traded my career as a professional warrior for one where I create peace in workplaces around the world. From law to peace!

The key was in losing my 'edges', my need for control and resistance against the flow of life, to rather follow the grand unfolding of who I am. No matter what decision I make, I know I can never get it wrong, because I have learned there is no failure. If I get an outcome I don't prefer, I check in with my state of being before making the next decision that will get me where I want to be. It is such a freeing way to exist and a concept I am taking around the world, one workplace at a time.

www.virginiarobin.com

Jaya McIntyre:Photograper

Jaya, an award-winning photographer, has dedicated her career to empowering women to help them feel comfortable behind the lens. With nearly three decades of experience, she has earned a stellar reputation as a professional, creative, and talented photographer. Jaya is the driving force behind Empire Art Photography, a renowned and thriving studio based on the Sunshine Coast.

Beyond her photography skills, Jaya is an advocate for the creative industries and small business owners. She strongly believes in recognizing and appreciating the expertise of masters of their craft. Her passion and dedication to her work are evident in her caring and focused approach.

Jaya's love for the Sunshine Coast, where she resides, is apparent in her daily life. When she's not capturing precious moments through her lens, she enjoys restaurant hopping with friends. Weekends are reserved for leisurely days spent along the pristine beaches with her husband, Terry.

Photography is not just a profession for Jaya; it is an inseparable part of her life. Through her work, Jaya has touched the lives of many and continues to inspire both aspiring photographers and women looking to embrace their own unique beauty.

www.empireartphotography.com.au

Roxanne McCarty-O'Kane: Writer

Since 2007 Roxanne's unique and multi-award winning method of storytelling has changed the lives of thousands of budding authors, allowing them to bring their messages to life in nonfiction books with structure, connection to the reader and potential profit. A prolific ghostwriter, author, workshop facilitator, writing mentor and journalist, Roxanne's presentations are charged with powerful content and tangible tools that remove the mystery from storytelling and ignite a thought-provoking and emotion-evoking theatre within the mind.

Her first book in the Ignite & Write series, *The Mindful Author,* has become a powerful resource for aspiring authors around the world to craft their manuscripts with confidence, clarity and a true sense of purpose and passion.

Roxanne is an award-winning businesswoman, recognised as the Sunshine Coast Micro/Small Businesswoman of the Year in 2021 and *The Mindful Author* was awarded first place in the 2023 International Reader Views Awards for Best Writing/Publishing Book.

As an MC, workshop facilitator and speaker, Roxanne's down to earth, relatable, humorous style engages her audience, inspires their minds and moves them to begin to think laterally about their own stories and how their lived experiences and knowledge journeys can have a greater impact on the world around them.

www.roxannewriter.com

Melinda Uys: Editor

Melinda is a versatile writer whose background in education, particularly teaching English and History, has fuelled her passion for crafting witty, meaningful words. Her innate desire to simplify and ease the lives of others has shaped her into the writer she is today. With a penchant for well-placed and beautiful language, Melinda has become a sought-after content and ghost writer, and editor.

Known for her ability to capture the essence and evoke emotions through her writing, Melinda's talent for painting vivid stories has garnered recognition across Sunshine Coast businesses, the state and internationally. Beyond her work as a writer, she is also an accomplished fiction writer, an avid travel writer, and a dedicated blogger.

Melinda resides near picturesque Noosa with her family, and shares her creative space with a beloved co-working cat named Trixie. With her skillful use of words and her unwavering passion for storytelling, Melinda continues to leave her mark in the writing world, connecting with readers and bringing their stories to life.

www.melindauys.com

A huge thank you to our creative team.

Talia Murray, Terry McIntyre, Shanti Martin, @melinadeemakeup, @thehairandmakeupartist_ @rawmakeupandhairstylist

Ladies, it's time to connect!

If you're looking for a dose of inspiration and empowerment, come join us at Women Inspired on social media. Our uplifting community is filled with incredible women who are breaking barriers, pursuing their dreams, and making a positive impact by sharing their story. We believe in the power of sisterhood and supporting each other's journeys. If you or someone you know would like to be a part of our next edition, we welcome you to reach out to us through our website. Together, let's celebrate the remarkable strength and potential within all of us.

www.womeninspired.com.au
www.facebook.com/womeninspired.com.au
www.instagram.com/womeninspiredaustralia/

www.ingramcontent.com/pod-product-compliance
Lightning Source LLC
Chambersburg PA
CBHW042030090426

42811CB00016B/1799